S0-BRM-777

LENT WITH POPE BENEDICT XVI

MEDITATIONS FOR EVERY DAY

3210 41st Street

Moline Public Library

Moline, IL 61265

Lent with Pope Benedict XVI

Meditations for Every Day

Compiled by Jeanne Kun

3 0067 00020 4183

theWORD
among us®
press

Copyright © 2012 Libreria Editrice Vaticana
Compilation Copyright © 2012 The Word Among Us Press

All rights reserved

Published by The Word Among Us Press
7115 Guilford Road
Frederick, Maryland 21704
www.wau.org

16 15 14 13 12   1 2 3 4 5

ISBN: 978-1-59325-198-7
eISBN: 978-1-59325-433-9

Scripture texts used in this work, as well as Pope Benedict XVI's homilies
and addresses, are taken from the Vatican translation and can be found on
the Vatican Web site, www.vatican.va. Used with permission of Libreria
Editrice Vaticana.

Cover design by John Hamilton Design
Cover photo © 2009 Getty Images

No part of this publication may be reproduced, stored in a retrieval system,
or transmitted in any form or by any means—electronic, mechanical,
photocopy, recording, or any other—except for brief quotations in printed
reviews, without the prior permission of the author and publisher.

Made and printed in the United States of America

Library of Congress Cataloging-in-Publication Data

Benedict XVI, Pope, 1927-
Lent with Pope Benedict XVI : meditations for every day / compiled by
Jeanne Kun.
  p. cm.
ISBN 978-1-59325-198-7 (alk. paper)
1. Lent--Prayers and devotions. 2. Catholic Church--Prayers and
devotions. I. Kun, Jeanne, 1951- II. Title.
BX2170.L4B46 2012
242'.34—dc23
                         2011034186

CONTENTS

PREFACE

The Lenten journey of forty days . . . is a favorable time
when the Church invites Christians to have a keener
awareness of the redeeming work of Christ
and to live their baptism in greater depth.
—Pope Benedict XVI, General Audience,
Ash Wednesday, March 1, 2006

The season of Lent is a collective retreat with our fellow Christians, during which we are urged to clear away the distractions and spiritual clutter in our lives and deepen our relationship with the Lord. It is a time to focus on conversion of heart and spiritual renewal. In fact, the word "Lent" fittingly comes from the Anglo-Saxon *lencten,* meaning "springtime" and sharing the same root as the word "lengthen." In the realm of nature, the hours of daylight become longer as winter turns into spring, a season of new births and new awakenings. So too, as we plant ourselves more deeply into Christ during this liturgical season of the Church year, will we experience spiritual enlightenment and new growth.

The reflections in this book have been chosen from homilies, messages, and addresses that Pope Benedict XVI has given during the Lenten seasons since the beginning of his pontificate, as well as from several of his encyclical letters. A reflection for each day of Lent is provided, as well as for the Triduum, Easter Day, and the Octave of Easter. These reflections are short enough to be read in a few minutes but deep enough to provide nourishment for an hour's worth of prayer and meditation. Pope Benedict is a gifted guide who will help us drink deeply from the well of Scripture in order to lead us to a deeper encounter with Christ.

With Pope Benedict accompanying us through Lent, may we come to a greater understanding and appreciation of all that has been won for us through Jesus' passion and death on the cross. And as we complete our journey and celebrate the risen Christ, may we be filled with profound gratitude and share in his joy and victory.

Jeanne Kun

A Call to Conversion

Today, Ash Wednesday, marks the beginning of the Church's Lenten journey toward Easter. Lent reminds us, as St. Paul exhorts, "not to accept the grace of God in vain" (cf. 2 Corinthians 6:1), but to recognize that today the Lord calls us to penance and spiritual renewal. This call to conversion is expressed in the two formulas used in the Rite of the Imposition of Ashes. The first formula—"Turn away from sin and be faithful to the Gospel"—echoes Jesus' words at the beginning of his public ministry (cf. Mark 1:15). It reminds us that conversion is meant to be a deep and lasting abandonment of our sinful ways in order to enter into a living relationship with Christ, who alone offers true freedom, happiness, and fulfillment. The second, older formula—"Remember, man, that you are dust, and to dust you shall return"—recalls the poverty and death which are the legacy of Adam's sin while pointing us to the resurrection, the new life, and the freedom brought by Christ, the Second Adam. This Lent, through the practice of prayer and penance and an ever more fruitful reception of the Church's sacraments, may we make our way to Easter with hearts purified and renewed by the grace of this special season.

—General Audience, Ash Wednesday, February 17, 2010

Thursday after Ash Wednesday

THE PATH OF TRUE HAPPINESS

Conversion is first and foremost a grace, a gift that opens the heart to God's infinite goodness. He himself anticipates with his grace our desire for conversion and accompanies our efforts for full adherence to his saving will. Therefore, to convert is to let oneself be won over by Jesus (cf. Philippians 3:12) and "to return" with him to the Father.

Conversion thus entails placing oneself humbly at the school of Jesus and walking meekly in his footsteps. In this regard, the words with which he himself points out the conditions for being his true disciples are enlightening. After affirming "Whoever would save his life will lose it; and whoever loses his life for my sake and the gospel's will save it," he adds, "For what does it profit a man, to gain the whole world and forfeit his life?" (Mark 8:35-36). To what extent does a life that is totally spent in achieving success, longing for prestige, and seeking commodities, to the point of excluding God from one's horizon, truly lead to happiness? Can true happiness exist when God is left out of consideration?

Experience shows that we are not happy because our material expectations and needs are satisfied. In fact, the only joy that fills the human heart is that which comes from God; indeed, we stand in need of infinite joy. Neither daily concerns nor life's difficulties succeed in extinguishing the joy that is born from friendship with God. Jesus' invitation to take up one's cross and follow him may at first sight seem harsh and contrary to what we hope for, mortifying our desire for personal fulfillment. At a closer look, however, we discover that it is not like this: The witness of the saints shows that in the cross of Christ, in the love that is given, in renouncing the possession of oneself, one finds that deep serenity which is the source of generous dedication to our brethren, especially to the poor and the needy, and this also gives us joy.

The Lenten journey of conversion on which we are setting out today, together with the entire Church, thus becomes a favorable opportunity, "the acceptable time" (2 Corinthians 6:2) for renewing our filial abandonment in the hands of God and for putting into practice what Jesus continues to repeat to us: "If any man would come after me, let him deny himself and take up his cross and follow me" (Mark 8:34). This is how one ventures forth on the path of love and true happiness.

—General Audience, Ash Wednesday, February 6, 2008

THE FORTY DAYS OF LENT

The Lenten journey of forty days . . . will lead us to the Easter Triduum, the memorial of the passion, death, and resurrection of the Lord, heart of the mystery of our salvation. It is a favorable time when the Church invites Christians to have a keener awareness of the redeeming work of Christ and to live their baptism in greater depth.

Indeed, in this liturgical season, the people of God from the earliest times have drawn abundant nourishment from the word of God to strengthen their faith, reviewing the entire history of creation and redemption. With its forty-day duration, Lent has an indisputably evocative power. Indeed, it intends to recall some of the events that marked the life and history of ancient Israel, presenting its paradigmatic value anew also to us. We think, for example, of the forty days of the great flood that led to God's covenant with Noah and, hence, with humanity, and of the forty days that Moses spent on Mount Sinai, after which he was given the tablets of the law.

The Lenten period is meant to serve as an invitation to relive with Jesus the forty days he spent in the desert, praying and fasting, in preparation for his public mission. Today, we too, together with all the world's Christians, are spiritually setting out toward

Calvary on a journey of reflection and prayer, meditating on the central mysteries of the faith. We will thus prepare ourselves to experience, after the mystery of the cross, the joy of Easter.

—General Audience, Ash Wednesday, March 1, 2006

LISTENING TO THE WORD OF TRUTH

The Christian's life is a life of faith, founded on the word of God and nourished by it. In the trials of life and in every temptation, the secret of victory lies in listening to the word of truth and rejecting with determination falsehood and evil.

This is the true and central program of the Lenten season: to listen to the word of truth; to live, speak, and do what is true; to refuse falsehood that poisons humanity and is the vehicle of all evils. It is therefore urgently necessary in these forty days to listen anew to the gospel, the word of the Lord, the word of truth, so that in every Christian, in every one of us, the understanding of the truth given to him, given to us, may be strengthened, so that we may live it and witness to it.

Lent encourages us to let the word of God penetrate our life and thus to know the fundamental truth: who we are, where we come from, where we must go, which road to take in life. And thus the season of Lent offers us an ascetic and liturgical route which, while helping us to open our eyes to our weaknesses, opens our hearts to the merciful love of Christ.

The Lenten journey, by bringing us close to God, enables us to look upon our brethren and their needs with new eyes. Those who begin to recognize God, to look at the face of Christ, also see their brother with other eyes—they discover their brother, what is good for him, what is bad for him, his needs. Lent, therefore, as a time of listening to the truth, is a favorable moment to convert to love, because the deep truth, the truth of God, is at the same time love. . . .

May these be days of reflection and of intense prayer, in which we let ourselves be guided by the word of God, which the liturgy offers to us in abundance. May Lent also be a time of fasting, penance, and watchfulness of ourselves, and may we be convinced that the fight against sin is never ending, because temptation is a daily reality and we all experience fragility and delusion.

Lastly, through almsgiving and doing good to others, may Lent be an opportunity for sincere sharing with our brethren of the gifts that we have received and of attention to the needs of the poorest and most abandoned people.

On this penitential journey, may we be accompanied by Mary, Mother of the Redeemer, who is a teacher of listening and of faithful adherence to God. May the Virgin Most Holy help us to arrive purified and renewed in mind and in spirit to celebrate the great mystery of Christ's Pasch.

—General Audience, Ash Wednesday, March 1, 2006

FIRST WEEK OF LENT

"Entering this liturgical season means continuously taking Christ's side against sin."

Deliverance from
the Slavery of Sin

This is the First Sunday of Lent, the liturgical season of forty days that constitutes a spiritual journey in the Church of preparation for Easter. Essentially, it is a matter of following Jesus, who is walking with determination toward the cross, the culmination of his mission of salvation. If we ask ourselves, "Why Lent? Why the cross?" the answer in radical terms is this: because evil exists, indeed sin, which according to the Scriptures is the profound cause of all evil. However, this affirmation is far from being taken for granted, and the very word "sin" is not accepted by many because it implies a religious vision of the world and of the human being.

In fact, it is true: If God is eliminated from the world's horizon, one cannot speak of sin. As when the sun is hidden, shadows disappear. Shadows only appear if the sun is out; hence, the eclipse of God necessarily entails the eclipse of sin.

Therefore, the sense of sin—which is something different from the "sense of guilt" as psychology understands it—is acquired by rediscovering the sense of God. This is expressed by the *Miserere*

Psalm, attributed to King David on the occasion of his double sin of adultery and homicide: "Against you," David says, addressing God, "against you only have I sinned" (Psalm 51:4).

In the face of moral evil, God's attitude is to oppose sin and to save the sinner. God does not tolerate evil because he is Love, Justice, and Fidelity; and for this very reason, he does not desire the death of the sinner but wants the sinner to convert and to live. To save humanity, God intervenes: We see him throughout the history of the Jewish people, beginning with the liberation from Egypt. God is determined to deliver his children from slavery in order to lead them to freedom. And the most serious and profound slavery is precisely that of sin.

For this reason, God sent his Son into the world: to set men and women free from the domination of Satan, "the origin and cause of every sin." God sent him in our mortal flesh so that he might become a victim of expiation, dying for us on the cross. The devil opposed this definitive and universal plan of salvation with all his might, as is shown in particular in the gospel of the temptation of Jesus in the wilderness, which is proclaimed every year on the First Sunday of Lent. In fact, entering this liturgical season means continuously taking Christ's side against sin, facing—both as individuals and as Church—the spiritual fight against the spirit of evil each time.

Let us therefore invoke the maternal help of Mary Most Holy for the Lenten journey that has just begun so that it may be rich in fruits of conversion.

—Angelus Address, First Sunday of Lent, March 13, 2011

OVERCOMING TEMPTATION

The Evangelist St. Luke recounts that after receiving baptism from John, "Jesus, full of the Holy Spirit, returned from the Jordan, and was led by the Spirit for forty days in the wilderness, tempted by the devil" (Luke 4:1-2). There is a clear insistence on the fact that the temptations were not just an incident on the way, but rather the consequence of Jesus' decision to carry out the mission entrusted to him by the Father—to live to the very end his reality as the beloved Son who trusts totally in him. Christ came into the world to set us free from sin and from the ambiguous fascination of planning our lives leaving God out. He did not do so with loud proclamations, but rather by fighting the tempter himself, until the cross. This example applies to everyone: The world is improved by starting with oneself, changing, with God's grace, everything in one's life that is not going well.

The first of the three temptations to which Satan subjects Jesus originates in hunger, that is, in material need: "If you are the Son of God, command this stone to become bread." But Jesus responds with sacred Scripture: "Man shall not live by bread alone" (Luke 4:3, 4; cf. Deuteronomy 8:3). Then the devil shows Jesus all the kingdoms of the earth and says: All this will be yours if, prostrating yourself, you worship me. This is the deception of power, and an attempt which Jesus was to unmask and reject: "You shall worship the Lord your God, and him only shall you serve" (cf. Luke 4:5, 8; Deuteronomy 6:13). Not adoration of power but only of God, of truth and love.

Lastly, the tempter suggests to Jesus that he work a spectacular miracle: that he throw himself down from the pinnacle of the Temple and let the angels save him so that everyone might believe in him. However, Jesus answers that God must never be put to the test (cf. Deuteronomy 6:16). We cannot "do an experiment" in which God has to respond and show that he is God: We must believe in him! We should not make God "the substance" of "our experiment." Still referring to sacred Scripture, Jesus puts the only authentic criterion—obedience, conformity to God's will, which is the foundation of our existence—before human criteria. This is also a fundamental teaching for us: If we carry God's word in our minds and hearts, if it enters our lives, if we trust in God, we can reject every kind of deception by the tempter. Furthermore, Christ's image as the new Adam emerges clearly from this account. He is the Son of God, humble and obedient to the Father, unlike Adam and Eve, who in the Garden of Eden succumbed to the seduction of the evil spirit, of being immortal without God.

Lent is like a long "retreat" in which to reenter oneself and listen to God's voice in order to overcome the temptations of the evil one and to find the truth of our existence. It is a time, we may say, of spiritual "training" in order to live alongside Jesus, not with pride and presumption, but rather by using the weapons of faith: namely, prayer, listening to the word of God, and penance. In this way we shall succeed in celebrating Easter in truth, ready to renew our baptismal promises.

—Angelus Address, First Sunday of Lent,
February 21, 2010

"Entering Lent"

L ast Wednesday we entered Lent with fasting and the Rite of Ashes. But what does "entering Lent" mean? It means we enter a season of special commitment in the spiritual battle to oppose the evil present in the world, in each one of us and around us. It means looking evil in the face and being ready to fight its effects and especially its causes—even its primary cause, which is Satan. It means not off-loading the problem of evil onto others, onto society, or onto God, but rather recognizing one's own responsibility and assuming it with awareness.

In this regard, Jesus' invitation to each one of us Christians to take up our "cross" and follow him with humility and trust (cf. Matthew 16:24) is particularly pressing. Although the "cross" may be heavy, it is not synonymous with misfortune, with disgrace, to be avoided on all accounts; rather, it is an opportunity to follow Jesus and thereby to acquire strength in the fight against sin and evil. Thus, "entering Lent" means renewing the personal and community decision to face evil together with Christ. The way of the cross is in fact the only way that leads to the victory of love over hatred, of sharing over selfishness, of peace over violence. Seen in this light, Lent is truly an opportunity for a strong ascetic and spiritual commitment based on Christ's grace.

—Angelus Address, First Sunday of Lent,
February 10, 2008

SPIRITUAL COMBAT

Every day, but particularly in Lent, Christians must face a struggle like the one that Christ underwent in the desert of Judea, where for forty days he was tempted by the devil, and then in Gethsemane, when he rejected the most severe temptation, accepting the Father's will to the very end. It is a spiritual battle waged against sin and, finally, against Satan. It is a struggle that involves the whole of the person and demands attentive and constant watchfulness.

St. Augustine remarks that those who want to walk in the love of God and in his mercy cannot be content with ridding themselves of grave and mortal sins but "should do the truth, also recognizing sins that are considered less grave . . . , and come to the light by doing worthy actions. Even less grave sins, if they are ignored, proliferate and produce death" (*In Io. evang.* 12, 13, 35).

Lent reminds us, therefore, that the Christian life is a never-ending combat in which the "weapons" of prayer, fasting, and penance are used. Fighting against evil, against every form of selfishness and hate, and dying to oneself to live in God is the ascetic journey that every disciple of Jesus is called to make with humility and patience, with generosity and perseverance.

Following the divine Teacher in docility makes Christians witnesses and apostles of peace.

We might say that this inner attitude also helps us to highlight more clearly what response Christians should give to the violence that is threatening peace in the world. It should certainly not be revenge, nor hatred, nor even flight into a false spiritualism. The response of those who follow Christ is rather to take the path chosen by the One who, in the face of the evils of his time and of all times, embraced the cross with determination, following the longer but more effective path of love. Following in his footsteps and united to him, we must all strive to oppose evil with good, falsehood with truth, and hatred with love.

—Homily, Ash Wednesday, March 1, 2006

THE VALUE OF FASTING

We might wonder what value and meaning there are for us Christians in depriving ourselves of something that in itself is good and useful for our bodily sustenance. The sacred Scriptures and the entire Christian tradition teach that fasting is a great help to avoid sin and all that leads to it. For this reason, the history of salvation is replete with occasions that invite fasting.

In the very first pages of sacred Scripture, the Lord commands man to abstain from partaking of the prohibited fruit: "You may freely eat of every tree of the garden; but of the tree of the knowledge of good and evil you shall not eat, for in the day that you eat of it you shall die" (Genesis 2:16-17). Commenting on the divine injunction, St. Basil observes that "fasting was ordained in Paradise" and that "the first commandment in this sense was delivered to Adam." He thus concludes: "'You shall not eat' is a law of fasting and abstinence" (cf. *Sermo de jejunio:* PG 31, 163, 98).

Since all of us are weighed down by sin and its consequences, fasting is proposed to us as an instrument to restore friendship with God. Such was the case with Ezra, who in preparation for the journey from exile back to the promised land, called upon the assembled people to fast so that "we might humble ourselves before our God" (Ezra 8:21). The Almighty heard their prayer and assured them of his favor and protection. In the same way, the people of Nineveh, responding to Jonah's call to repentance, proclaimed a fast as a sign of their sincerity, saying, "Who knows, God may yet repent and turn from his fierce anger, so that we perish not?" (Jonah 3:9). In this instance too, God saw their works and spared them.

In the New Testament, Jesus brings to light the profound motive for fasting, condemning the attitude of the Pharisees, who scrupulously observed the prescriptions of the law but whose hearts were far from God. True fasting, as the divine Master repeats elsewhere, is rather to do the will of the heavenly Father, who "sees in secret, and will reward you" (Matthew 6:18). He himself sets the example, answering Satan at the end of the forty days spent in the desert that "man shall not live by bread alone, but by every word that proceeds from the mouth of God" (Matthew 4:4). The true fast is thus directed to eating the "true food," which is to do the Father's will (cf. John 4:34). If, therefore, Adam disobeyed the Lord's command "of the tree of the knowledge of good and evil you shall not eat," the believer, through fasting, intends to submit himself humbly to God, trusting in his goodness and mercy.

The practice of fasting is very present in the first Christian community (cf. Acts 13:3; 14:23; 2 Corinthians 6:5). The

Church fathers, too, speak of the force of fasting to bridle sin, especially the lusts of the "old Adam," and open in the heart of the believer a path to God. Moreover, fasting is a practice that is encountered frequently and recommended by the saints of every age. St. Peter Chrysologus writes: "Fasting is the soul of prayer, mercy is the lifeblood of fasting. So if you pray, fast; if you fast, show mercy; if you want your petition to be heard, hear the petition of others. If you do not close your ear to others, you open God's ear to yourself" (*Sermo* 43: PL 52, 320, 322).

—Message for Lent 2009

ALMSGIVING:
THE GENEROSITY OF LOVE

Almsgiving teaches us the generosity of love. St. Joseph Benedict Cottolengo forthrightly recommends: "Never keep an account of the coins you give, since this is what I always say: If, in giving alms, the left hand is not to know what the right hand is doing, then the right hand, too, should not know what it does itself" (*Detti e pensieri,* Edilibri, n. 201).

In this regard, all the more significant is the gospel story of the widow who, out of her poverty, cast into the Temple treasury "all she had to live on" (Mark 12:44). Her tiny and insignificant coin becomes an eloquent symbol: This widow gives to God, not out of her abundance, not so much what she has, but what she is—her entire self. We find this moving passage inserted in the description of the days that immediately precede the passion and death of Jesus, who, as St. Paul writes, made himself poor to enrich us out of his poverty (cf. 2 Corinthians 8:9). He gave his entire self for us.

Lent, also through the practice of almsgiving, inspires us to follow Jesus' example. In his school we can learn to make of our lives a total gift; imitating him, we are able to make ourselves available, not so much in giving a part of what we possess, but our very selves. Cannot the entire gospel be summarized perhaps in the one commandment of love? The Lenten practice of alms-giving thus becomes a means to deepen our Christian vocation. In gratuitously offering himself, the Christian bears witness that it is love and not material richness that determines the laws of his existence. Love, then, gives almsgiving its value; it inspires various forms of giving, according to the possibilities and conditions of each person.

Dear brothers and sisters, Lent invites us to "train ourselves" spiritually, also through the practice of almsgiving, in order to grow in charity and recognize in the poor Christ himself. In the Acts of the Apostles, we read that the apostle Peter said to the cripple who was begging alms at the Temple gate: "I have no silver or gold, but what I have I give you; in the name of Jesus Christ the Nazarene, walk" (3:6). In giving alms we offer something material, a sign of the greater gift that we can impart to others through the announcement and witness of Christ, in whose name is found true life. Let this time, then, be marked by a personal and community effort of attachment to Christ in order that we may be witnesses of his love.

—Message for Lent 2008

What It Means to Follow Christ

The expression "following of Christ" is a description of the whole of Christian existence. In what does it consist? What does "to follow Christ" actually mean? At the outset, with the first disciples, its meaning was very simple and immediate: It meant that to go with Jesus, these people decided to give up their profession, their affairs, their whole life. It meant undertaking a new profession: discipleship. The fundamental content of this profession was accompanying the Teacher and total entrustment to his guidance. The "following" was therefore something external but, at the same time very internal. The exterior aspect was walking behind Jesus on his journeys through Palestine. The interior aspect was the new existential orientation whose reference points were no longer in events, in work as a source of income, or in the personal will, but in total abandonment to the will of Another. Being at his disposal, henceforth, became the *raison d'être* of life.

In certain gospel scenes, we can recognize quite clearly that this means the renouncement of one's possessions and detachment from oneself. But with this, it is also clear what "following" means for us and what its true essence is for us: It is an interior change of life. It requires me to be no longer withdrawn into myself, considering my own fulfillment the main reason for my life. It requires me to give myself freely to Another—for truth, for love, for God who, in Jesus Christ, goes before me and shows me the way.

It is a question of the fundamental decision to no longer consider usefulness and gain, my career and success, as the ultimate goals of my life, but instead to recognize truth and love as authentic criteria. It is a question of choosing between living only for myself or giving myself for what is greater. And let us understand properly that truth and love are not abstract values; in Jesus Christ they have become a Person. By following him I enter into the service of truth and love. By losing myself I find myself.

—Homily, Palm Sunday of the Passion of Our Lord,
April 1, 2007

SECOND WEEK OF LENT

"To enter eternal life requires listening to Jesus, following him on the way of the cross, carrying in our hearts like him the hope of the resurrection."

TRANSFIGURED IN HOPE

Today is the Second Sunday of Lent. As we continue on the penitential journey, the liturgy invites us, after presenting the gospel of Jesus' temptations in the desert last week, to reflect on the extraordinary event of the transfiguration on the mountain. Considered together, these episodes anticipate the paschal mystery: Jesus' struggle with the tempter preludes the great final duel of the passion, while the light of his transfigured body anticipates the glory of the resurrection. On the one hand, we see Jesus, fully man, sharing with us even temptation; on the other, we contemplate him as the Son of God who divinizes our humanity. Thus, we could say that these two Sundays serve as pillars on which to build the entire structure of Lent until Easter and, indeed, the entire structure of Christian life, which consists essentially in paschal dynamism: from death to life.

The mountain—Mount Tabor, like Sinai—is the place of nearness to God. Compared with daily life, it is the lofty space in which to breathe the pure air of creation. It is the place of prayer in which to stand in the Lord's presence, like Moses and Elijah, who appeared beside the transfigured Jesus and spoke to him of the "exodus" that awaited him in Jerusalem, that is, his Pasch. The transfiguration is a prayer event: In praying, Jesus is immersed in God, closely united to him, adhering with his own human will to the loving will of the Father. And thus light invades him and appears visibly as the truth of his being: He is God, Light of Light.

Even Jesus' raiment becomes dazzling white. This is reminiscent of the white garment worn by neophytes. Those who are reborn in baptism are clothed in light, anticipating heavenly existence (cf. Revelation 7:9, 13). This is the crucial point: The transfiguration is an anticipation of the resurrection, but this presupposes death. Jesus expresses his glory to the apostles so that they may have the strength to face the scandal of the cross and understand that it is necessary to pass through many tribulations in order to reach the kingdom of God. The Father, whose voice resounds from on high, proclaims Jesus his beloved Son as he did at the baptism in the Jordan, adding, "Listen to him" (Matthew 17:5). To enter eternal life requires listening to Jesus, following him on the way of the cross, carrying in our hearts like him the hope of the resurrection. "*Spe salvi*," "saved in hope." Today we can say: "Transfigured in hope."

Turning now in prayer to Mary, let us recognize in her the human creature transfigured within by Christ's grace and entrust ourselves to her guidance to walk joyfully on our path through Lent.

—Angelus Address, Second Sunday of Lent,
February 17, 2008

LIGHT FROM LIGHT

After Jesus had foretold his passion to the disciples, he "took with him Peter and James and John his brother, and led them up a high mountain apart. And he was transfigured before them, and his face shone like the sun, and his garments became white as light" (Matthew 17:1-2). According to the senses, the light of the sun is the brightest light known in nature, but according to the spirit, the disciples briefly glimpsed an even more intense splendor—that of the divine glory of Jesus, which illumines the whole history of salvation. St. Maximus Confessor says that "[the Lord's] garments appear white, that is to say, the words of the gospel will then be clear and distinct, with nothing concealed" (*Ambiguum* 10: PG 91, 1128 B).

The gospel tells us that beside the transfigured Jesus, "there appeared . . . Moses and Elijah, talking with him" (Matthew 17:3), Moses and Elijah, figures of the law and of the prophets. It was then that Peter, ecstatic, exclaimed: "Lord, it is well that we are here; if you wish, I will make three booths here, one for you and one for Moses and one for Elijah" (17:4). However, as St. Augustine commented, we have only one dwelling place, Christ: "He is the Word of God, the Word of God in the Law, the Word of God in the Prophets" (*Sermo De Verbis Ev.* 78:3: PL 38, 491).

In fact, the Father himself proclaims: "This is my beloved Son, with whom I am well pleased; listen to him" (Matthew 17:5). The transfiguration is not a change in Jesus but the revelation of his divinity: "the profound interpenetration of his being with God, which then becomes pure light. In his oneness with the Father, Jesus is himself 'light from light'" (*Jesus of Nazareth: From the Baptism in the Jordan to the Transfiguration*, Doubleday, New York, 2007, p. 310).

Peter, James, and John, contemplating the divinity of the Lord, are ready to face the scandal of the cross, as it is sung in an ancient hymn: "You were transfigured on the mountain, and your disciples, insofar as they were able, contemplated your glory, in order that, on seeing you crucified, they would understand that your passion was voluntary and proclaim to the world that you are truly the splendor of the Father."

Dear friends, let us, too, share in this vision and in this supernatural gift, making room for prayer and for listening to the word of God.

—Angelus Address, Second Sunday of Lent,
March 20, 2011

PRAYING IN THE LIGHT OF CHRIST

T he transfiguration of Jesus was essentially an experience of prayer (cf. Luke 9:28-29). Indeed, prayer reaches its culmination and thus becomes a source of inner light when the spirit of the human being adheres to that of God and their respective wills merge, as it were, to become a whole. When Jesus went up the mountain, he was immersed in contemplation of the loving plan of the Father, who had sent him into the world to save humanity. Elijah and Moses appeared beside Jesus, meaning that the sacred Scriptures were in concordance with the proclamation of his paschal mystery—that, in other words, Christ had to suffer and die in order to enter into his glory (cf. Luke 24:26, 46). At that moment Jesus saw silhouetted before him the cross, the extreme sacrifice necessary in order to free us from the dominion of sin and death. And in his heart, once again, he repeated his "Amen." He said, "Yes, here I am; may your loving will be done, O Father." And as had happened after his baptism in the Jordan, from heaven there came signs of God the Father's pleasure: the light that transfigured Christ and the voice that proclaimed him "my beloved Son" (Mark 9:7).

Together with fasting and works of mercy, prayer is the backbone of our spiritual life. Dear brothers and sisters, I urge you to find in this Lenten season prolonged moments of silence, possibly in retreat, in order to review your own lives in the light of the loving plan of the heavenly Father. Let yourselves be guided in this more intense listening to God by the Virgin Mary, a teacher and model of prayer. Even in the thick darkness of Christ's passion, she did not lose the light of her divine Son but rather treasured it in her heart. For this we call on her as Mother of Trust and Hope!

—Angelus Address, Second Sunday of Lent, March 8, 2009

DARING TO SAY YES TO GOD

He who loves his life loses it, and he who hates his life in this world will keep it for eternal life" (John 12:25). In other words, the one who wants to have his life for himself—living only for himself, keeping everything to himself and exploiting all its possibilities—is actually the one who loses his life. Life becomes boring and empty. Only by self-abandonment, only by the disinterested gift of the "I" in favor of the "you," only in the "yes" to the greater life, the life of God, does our life also become broad and great. Thus, this fundamental principle established by the Lord is ultimately identical to the principle of love. Love, in fact, means letting go of oneself, giving oneself, not wanting to possess oneself, but becoming free from oneself. It means not retiring into oneself—("What will become of me?")—but looking ahead, toward the other, toward God and the men that he sends to me. And once again, this principle of love, which defines man's path, is identical to the mystery of the cross, to the mystery of death and resurrection that we encounter in Christ.

Dear friends, perhaps it is relatively easy to accept this as the fundamental great vision of life. In practice, however, it is not a question of simply recognizing a principle, but of living according to the truth that it contains, the truth of the cross and resurrection. Hence, once again, a single great decision is not enough. It is certainly important; it is essential to dare to take the great fundamental decision once, to dare to utter the great "yes" that the Lord asks of us at a certain moment of our lives. But the great yes of the decisive moment in our life—the yes to the truth that the Lord puts before us—must then be won afresh every day in the situations of daily life when we have to abandon our "I" over and over again, placing ourselves at the Lord's disposal when deep down we would prefer to cling to our "I."

An upright life always involves sacrifice, renunciation. To hold out the promise of a life without this constant re-giving of self is to mislead. There is no such thing as a successful life without sacrifice. If I cast a glance back over my whole life, I have to say that it was precisely the moments when I said yes to renunciation that were the great and important moments of my life.

—Homily, Palm Sunday of the Passion of Our Lord,
April 5, 2009

Preparing for the Fight

Fasting, to which the Church invites us in this particular season, certainly is not motivated by the physical or aesthetical order, but stems from the need that man has for an interior purification that detoxifies him from the pollution of sin and evil. It educates him to that healthy renunciation that releases the believer from the slavery to self; that renders him more attentive and open to listen to God and to be at the service of the brethren. For this reason, fasting and the other Lenten practices are considered the traditional Christian spiritual "arms" used to fight evil, unhealthy passions, and vice. Concerning this, I would like to listen, together with you, to a brief commentary by St. John Chrysostom:

As at the end of winter, the summer season returns, and the navigator launches his boat into the sea; the soldier polishes his arms and trains the horse for battle; the farmer sharpens the scythe; the wayfarer, strengthened, continues his journey; and the athlete sets aside his vestments and prepares for the race. So we, too, at the start of this fast, like returning to a spiritual springtime, we polish the arms like the soldier; we sharpen the scythe like the farmers; and as mariners we launch the boat of our spirit to confront the waves of senseless passions; like the wayfarer we continue the journey to heaven; and as the athlete we prepare ourselves for the fight by totally setting aside everything. (cf. Homily to the People of Antioch, n. 3).

In the Message for Lent, I extended the invitation to live these forty days of special grace as a "Eucharistic" time. Drawing from the inexhaustible font of love that the Eucharist is, in which Christ renews the redemptive sacrifice of the cross, each Christian can persevere on the journey.

The works of charity (almsgiving), prayer, fasting, together with every sincere effort of conversion, find their most lofty significance and value in the Eucharist, center and culmination of the life of the Church and the history of salvation.

"May this Sacrament that we have received, O Father," we will pray at the end of Holy Mass, "sustain us on our Lenten way, make holy our fasting, and render it efficacious to heal our spirit." We ask Mary to accompany us so that at the end of Lent, we may contemplate the risen Lord, interiorly renewed and reconciled with God and our brethren. Amen!

—Homily, Ash Wednesday, February 21, 2007

THE HUMILITY OF CHRIST

May divine grace open our hearts to an understanding of the invaluable gift of salvation, obtained for us by Christ's sacrifice. We find this immense gift wonderfully described in a famous hymn contained in the Letter to the Philippians (cf. 2:6-11). . . .

The apostle Paul concisely and effectively retraces the mystery of the history of salvation, mentioning the arrogance of Adam, who, although he was not God, wanted to be like God. And he compares the arrogance of the first man, which we all tend to feel in our being, with the humility of the true Son of God, who, in becoming man, does not hesitate to take upon himself all human weaknesses save sin, and goes even so far as the depths of death. This descent to the ultimate depths of the passion and death is followed by his exaltation, the true glory, the glory of love which went to the very end. And it is therefore right, as St. Paul says, that "at Jesus' name every knee must bend in the heavens, on the earth and under the earth, and every tongue profess that Jesus Christ is Lord" (Philippians 2:10-11). With these words St. Paul refers to a prophecy of Isaiah in which God says: I am God. . . . To me every knee shall bend in heaven and on earth (cf. Isaiah 45:22, 23). This, Paul says, applies to Jesus

Christ. He truly is, in his humility, in the true greatness of his love, the Lord of the world, and before him every knee bends.

How marvelous and, at the same time, surprising this mystery is! We can never sufficiently meditate on this reality. In spite of being God, Jesus does not want to make his divine prerogative an exclusive possession; he does not want to use his being as God, his glorious dignity and his power, as an instrument of triumph and a sign of remoteness from us. On the contrary, "he empties himself," taking on the wretched and weak human condition. In this regard, Paul uses a rather evocative Greek verb to indicate the *kénosis,* this humbling of Jesus. In Christ the divine form (*morphé*) was hidden beneath the human form, that is, beneath our reality marked by suffering, by poverty, by our human limitations, and by death. His radical, true sharing in our nature, a sharing in all things save sin, led him to that boundary which is the sign of our finiteness: death. However, all this was not the fruit of an obscure mechanism or blind fatality; rather, it was his own free choice through generous adherence to the Father's saving plan. And the death he went to meet, Paul adds, was that of crucifixion, the most humiliating and degrading death imaginable. The Lord of the universe did all this out of love for us; out of love he chose "to empty himself" and make himself our brother; out of love he shared our condition, that of every man and every woman.

—General Audience, April 8, 2009

EYES FIXED ON CHRIST

They shall look on him whom they have pierced" (John 19:37). The beloved disciple, present at Calvary together with Mary, the Mother of Jesus, and some other women, was an eyewitness to the thrust of the lance that passed through Christ's side, causing blood and water to flow forth (cf. John 19:31-34). That gesture by an anonymous Roman soldier, destined to be lost in oblivion, remains impressed on the eyes and heart of the apostle, who takes it up in his gospel. How many conversions have come about down the centuries thanks to the eloquent message of love that the one who looks upon Jesus crucified receives!

Therefore, we enter into the Lenten season with our "gaze" fixed on the side of Jesus. In the Encyclical Letter *Deus Caritas Est* (cf. 12), I wished to emphasize that only by looking at Jesus dead on the cross for us can this fundamental truth be known and contemplated: "God is love" (1 John 4:8, 16). "In this contemplation," I wrote, "the Christian discovers the path along which his life and love must move" (12).

Contemplating the crucified One with the eyes of faith, we can understand in depth what sin is, how tragic is its gravity, and at the same time how immense is the Lord's power of forgiveness and mercy. During these days of Lent, let us not distance our hearts from this mystery of profound humanity and lofty spirituality. Looking at Christ, we feel at the same time looked at by him. He whom we have pierced with our faults never tires of pouring out upon the world an inexhaustible torrent of merciful love.

May humankind understand that only from this font is it possible to draw the indispensable spiritual energy to build that peace and happiness which every human being continually seeks. Let us ask the Virgin Mary, pierced in spirit next to the cross of her Son, to obtain for us a solid faith. Guiding us along the Lenten journey, may she help us to leave all that distances us from listening to Christ and his saving word.

—Angelus Address, First Sunday of Lent,
February 25, 2007

THIRD WEEK OF LENT

*"God thirsts for our faith and our love.
As a good and merciful father, he wants our
total possible good, and this good is
he himself."*

QUENCHING OUR THIRST

This year [Cycle A] on this Third Sunday of Lent, the liturgy again presents one of the most beautiful and profound passages of the Bible: the dialogue between Jesus and the Samaritan woman (cf. John 4:5-42). . . . It is impossible to give a brief explanation of the wealth of this gospel passage. One must read and meditate on it personally, identifying oneself with that woman who, one day like so many other days, went to draw water from the well and found Jesus there, sitting next to it, "tired from the journey" in the midday heat. "Give me a drink," he said, leaving her very surprised: It was, in fact, completely out of the ordinary that a Jew would speak to a Samaritan woman, and all the more so to a stranger. But the woman's bewilderment was destined to increase. Jesus spoke of a "living water" able to quench her thirst and become in her "a spring of water welling up to eternal life." In addition, he demonstrated that he knew her personal life; he revealed that the hour had come to adore the one true God in spirit and truth; and finally, he entrusted her with something extremely rare: He told her that he is the Messiah.

All this began from the real and notable experience of thirst. The theme of thirst runs throughout John's Gospel: from the meeting with the Samaritan woman to the great prophecy during the feast of Tabernacles (7:37-38) and even to the cross, when Jesus, before he dies, in order to fulfill the Scriptures, says, "I thirst" (19:28). Christ's thirst is an entranceway to the mystery of God, who became thirsty to satisfy our thirst, just as he became poor to make us rich (cf. 2 Corinthians 8:9). Yes, God thirsts for our faith and our love. As a good and merciful father, he wants our total possible good, and this good is he himself. The Samaritan woman, on the other hand, represents the existential dissatisfaction of one who does not find what he seeks. She has had "five husbands," and now she lives with another man; her going to and from the well to draw water expresses a repetitive and resigned life. However, everything changes for her that day thanks to the conversation with the Lord Jesus, who upsets her to the point that she leaves her pitcher of water and runs to tell the villagers: "Come, see a man who told me all that I ever did. Can this be the Christ?" (John 4:29).

Dear brothers and sisters, like the Samaritan woman, let us also open our hearts to listen trustingly to God's word in order to encounter Jesus who reveals his love to us and tells us, "I who speak to you am he" (John 4:26), the Messiah, your Savior. May Mary, the first and most perfect disciple of the Word made flesh, obtain this gift for us.

—Angelus Address, Third Sunday of Lent,
February 24, 2008

THE NEED TO CHANGE

R epent,' says the Lord, 'for the kingdom of heaven is at hand,'" we proclaimed before the gospel of this Third Sunday of Lent [Cycle C], which presents us with the fundamental theme of this "strong season" of the liturgical year: the invitation to change our lives and to do works worthy of penance. Jesus, as we heard, recalls two items of news: a brutal repression in the Temple by the Roman police (cf. Luke 13:1) and the tragic death of eighteen people, killed when the tower in Siloam collapsed (13:4). People interpret these events as divine punishment for those victims' sins and, thinking they are upright, believe they are safe from such accidents and that they have nothing in their own lives that they should change.

Jesus, however, denounces this attitude as an illusion: "Do you think that these Galileans were worse sinners than all the other Galileans, because they suffered thus? I tell you, No; but unless you repent you will all likewise perish" (Luke 13:2-3). And he invites us to reflect on these events for a greater commitment on the journey of conversion, for it is precisely the closure of ourselves to the Lord and the failure to take the path of our own conversion that lead to death, to the death of the soul. In Lent each one of us is asked by God to mark a turning point in our life, thinking and living in accordance with the gospel, correcting some aspect of our way of praying, acting, or working and of our relations with others. Jesus makes this appeal to us, not with a severity that is an end in itself, but precisely because he is concerned for our good, our happiness, and our salvation. For our part, we must respond to him with a sincere inner effort, asking him to make us understand which particular ways we should change.

The conclusion of the gospel passage reverts to the prospect of mercy, showing the urgent need to return to God, to renew life in accordance with God. Referring to a custom of the time, Jesus presents the parable of a fig tree planted in the vineyard. However, this fig tree was barren; it produced no fruit (cf. Luke 13:6-9). The dialogue that develops between the master and the vinedresser shows, on the one hand, the mercy of God, who is patient and allows human beings—all of us—time in which to convert; and on the other, the need to start to change both our interior and exterior way of life straight away in order not to miss the opportunities that God's mercy affords us to overcome our spiritual laziness and respond to God's love with our own filial love.

—Homily, Third Sunday of Lent, March 7, 2010

FAITH IS BORN FROM ENCOUNTER

God thirsts for our faith and wants us to find the source of our authentic happiness in him. Every believer is in danger of practicing a false religiosity, of not seeking in God the answer to the most intimate expectations of the heart but, on the contrary, treating God as though he were at the service of our desires and projects. . . .

The symbolism of water returns with great eloquence in the famous gospel passage that recounts Jesus' meeting with the Samaritan woman in Sychar by Jacob's well. We immediately perceive a link between the well, built by the great patriarch of Israel to guarantee his family water, and salvation history, where God gives humanity water welling up to eternal life. If there is a physical thirst for water that is indispensable for life on this earth, there is also a spiritual thirst in man that God alone can satisfy.

This is clearly visible in the dialogue between Jesus and the woman who came to Jacob's well to draw water. Everything begins with Jesus' request: "Give me a drink" (cf. John 4:5-7). At first sight it seems a simple request for a little water in the hot midday sun. In fact, with this question, addressed moreover to a Samaritan woman—there was bad blood between the Jews and the Samaritans—Jesus triggers in the woman to whom he is talking an inner process that kindles within her the desire for something more profound. St. Augustine comments, "Although Jesus asked for a drink, his real thirst was for this woman's faith" (*In Io ev. Tract.* XV, 11: PL 35, 1514). In fact, at a certain point, it was the woman herself who asked Jesus for the water (cf. John 4:15), thereby demonstrating that in every person there is an inherent need for God and for salvation that only God can satisfy. It is a thirst for the infinite which only the water that Jesus offers, the living water of the Spirit, can quench. In a little while, in the Preface, we shall hear these words: Jesus "asked the woman of Samaria for water to drink, and had already prepared for her the gift of faith. In his thirst to receive her faith, he awakened in her heart the fire of your love."

Dear brothers and sisters, in this dialogue between Jesus and the Samaritan woman, we see outlined the spiritual itinerary that each one of us, that every Christian community, is ceaselessly called to rediscover and follow. . . . As he did with the Samaritan woman, Jesus wishes to bring us to profess our faith powerfully in him so that we may then proclaim and witness to our brethren the joy of the encounter with him and the marvels that his love works in our existence. Faith is born from the encounter with Jesus, recognized and accepted as the definitive Revealer and Savior in whom God's face is revealed. Once the Lord has won the Samaritan woman's heart, her life is transformed and she runs without delay to take the good news to her people (cf. John 4:28-29).

—Homily, Third Sunday of Lent, February 24, 2008

GOD IS LOVE

God is love, and he who abides in love abides in God, and God abides in him" (1 John 4:16). These words from the First Letter of John express with remarkable clarity the heart of the Christian faith: the Christian image of God, and the resulting image of mankind and its destiny. In the same verse, St. John also offers a kind of summary of the Christian life: "We have come to know and to believe in the love God has for us."

We have come to believe in God's love. In these words the Christian can express the fundamental decision of his life. Being Christian is not the result of an ethical choice or a lofty idea, but the encounter with an event, a person, which gives life a new horizon and a decisive direction. St. John's Gospel describes that event in these words: "God so loved the world that he gave his only Son, that whoever believes in him should . . . have eternal life" (3:16). In acknowledging the centrality of love, Christian faith has retained the core of Israel's faith while at the same time giving it new depth and breadth. The pious Jew prayed daily the words of the Book of Deuteronomy, which expressed the heart of his existence: "Hear, O Israel: the LORD our God is one LORD; and you shall love the LORD your God with all your heart, and with all your soul, and with all your might" (6:4-5). Jesus united into a single precept this commandment of love for God and the commandment of love for neighbor found in the Book of Leviticus: "You shall love your neighbor as yourself" (19:18; cf. Mark 12:29-31). Since God has first loved us (cf. 1 John 4:10), love is now no longer a mere "command"; it is the response to the gift of love with which God draws near to us.

—Encyclical *Deus Caritas Est*, 1-2

FASTING OPENS OUR EYES

T he faithful practice of fasting contributes . . . to conferring unity to the whole person, body and soul, helping to avoid sin and grow in intimacy with the Lord. St. Augustine, who knew all too well his own negative impulses, defining them as "twisted and tangled knottiness" (*Confessions,* II, 10.18), writes: "I will certainly impose privation, but it is so that he will forgive me, to be pleasing in his eyes, that I may enjoy his delightfulness" (*Sermo* 400, 3, 3: PL 40, 708). Denying material food, which nourishes our body, nurtures an interior disposition to listen to Christ and be fed by his saving word. Through fasting and praying, we allow him to come and satisfy the deepest hunger that we experience in the depths of our being: the hunger and thirst for God.

At the same time, fasting is an aid to open our eyes to the situation in which so many of our brothers and sisters live. In his first letter, St. John admonishes: "If anyone has the world's goods and sees his brother in need, yet shuts up his bowels of compassion from him, how does the love of God abide in him?" (1 John 3:17). Voluntary fasting enables us to grow in the spirit of the Good Samaritan, who bends low and goes to the help of his suffering brother (cf. *Deus Caritas Est,* 15). By freely embracing an act of self-denial for the sake of another, we make a statement that our brother or sister in need is not a stranger.

It is precisely to keep alive this welcoming and attentive attitude toward our brothers and sisters that I encourage the parishes and every other community to intensify in Lent the custom of private and communal fasts, joined to the reading of the word of God, prayer, and almsgiving. From the beginning this has been the hallmark of the Christian community, in which special collections were taken up (cf. 2 Corinthians 8–9; Romans 15:25-27), the faithful being invited to give to the poor what had been set aside from their fast (*Didascalia Ap.*, V, 20, 18). This practice needs to be rediscovered and encouraged again in our day, especially during the liturgical season of Lent.

—Message for Lent 2009

LET US BECOME FRIENDS OF JESUS

This is eternal life, that they may know you the only true God, and Jesus Christ, whom you have sent" (John 17:3). Everyone wants to have life. We long for a life which is authentic, complete, worthwhile, full of joy. This yearning for life coexists with a resistance to death, which nonetheless remains inescapable. When Jesus speaks about eternal life, he is referring to real and true life, a life worthy of being lived. He is not simply speaking about life after death. He is talking about authentic life, a life fully alive and thus not subject to death, yet one which can already—and indeed must—begin in this world. Only if we learn even now how to live authentically, if we learn how to live the life which death cannot take away, does the promise of eternity become meaningful.

But how does this happen? What is this true and eternal life which death cannot touch? We have heard Jesus' answer: *This is eternal life, that they may know you—God—and the one whom you have sent, Jesus Christ.* Much to our surprise, we are told that life is knowledge. This means, first of all, that life is relationship. No one has life from himself and only for himself. We have it from others and in a relationship with others.

If it is a relationship in truth and love, a giving and receiving, it gives fullness to life and makes it beautiful.

But for that very reason, the destruction of that relationship by death can be especially painful; it can put life itself in question. Only a relationship with the One who is himself Life can preserve my life beyond the floodwaters of death, can bring me through them alive. Already in Greek philosophy, we encounter the idea that man can find eternal life if he clings to what is indestructible—to truth, which is eternal. He needs, as it were, to be full of truth in order to bear within himself the stuff of eternity. But only if truth is a Person can it lead me through the night of death. We cling to God—to Jesus Christ the Risen One. And thus, we are led by the One who is himself Life. In this relationship we, too, live by passing through death, since we are not forsaken by the One who is himself Life.

But let us return to Jesus' words: *This is eternal life: that they know you and the One whom you have sent*. Knowledge of God becomes eternal life. Clearly "knowledge" here means something more than mere factual knowledge as, for example, when we know that a famous person has died or a discovery has been made. Knowing, in the language of sacred Scripture, is an interior becoming one with the other. Knowing God, knowing Christ, always means loving him, becoming, in a sense, one with him by virtue of that knowledge and love. Our life becomes authentic and true life, and thus eternal life, when we know the

One who is the source of all being and all life. And so Jesus' words become a summons: Let us become friends of Jesus; let us try to know him all the more! Let us live in dialogue with him! Let us learn from him how to live aright; let us be his witnesses! Then we become people who love, and then we act aright. Then we are truly alive.

—Homily, Holy Thursday, April 1, 2010

FOR GOD'S GLORY, NOT OUR OWN

The gospel highlights a typical feature of Christian alms-giving: It must be hidden. "Do not let your left hand know what your right hand is doing," Jesus asserts, "so that your alms may be in secret" (Matthew 6:3-4). Just a short while before, he said not to boast of one's own good works so as not to risk being deprived of the heavenly reward (cf. 6:1-2). The disciple is to be concerned with God's greater glory. Jesus warns, "In this way, let your light shine before others, so that they may see your good works and give glory to your Father in heaven" (5:16). Everything, then, must be done for God's glory and not our own.

This understanding, dear brothers and sisters, must accompany every gesture of help to our neighbor so that it does not become a means for making ourselves the center of attention. If in accomplishing a good deed, we do not have as our goal God's glory and the real well-being of our brothers and sisters, looking rather for a return of personal interest or simply of applause, then we place ourselves outside of the gospel vision.

In today's world of images, attentive vigilance is required, since this temptation is great. Almsgiving, according to the gospel, is not mere philanthropy; rather, it is a concrete expression of charity, a theological virtue that demands interior conversion to love of God and neighbor in imitation of Jesus Christ, who, dying on the cross, gave his entire self for us. How could we not thank God for the many people who silently, far from the gaze of the media world, fulfill, with this spirit, generous actions in support of one's neighbor in difficulty? There is little use in giving one's personal goods to others if it leads to a heart puffed up in vainglory. For this reason, the one who knows that God "sees in secret" and in secret will reward does not seek human recognition for works of mercy.

—Message for Lent 2008

FOURTH WEEK OF LENT

*"The Lenten journey that we are taking
is a special time of grace during which we
can experience the gift of the Lord's
kindness to us."*

Fourth Sunday of Lent

The Light of Faith

The Lenten journey that we are taking is a special time of grace during which we can experience the gift of the Lord's kindness to us. The liturgy of this Sunday, called "Laetare," invites us to be glad and rejoice as the entrance antiphon of the Eucharistic celebration proclaims: "Rejoice, Jerusalem! Be glad for her, you who love her; rejoice with her, you who mourned for her, and you will find contentment at her consoling breasts" (cf. Isaiah 66:10-11).

What is the profound reason for this joy? Today's gospel, in which Jesus heals a man blind from birth, tells us. The question that the Lord Jesus asks the blind man is the high point of the story: "Do you believe in the Son of man?" (John 9:35). The man recognizes the sign worked by Jesus, and he passes from the light of his eyes to the light of faith: "Lord, I believe!" (9:38).

It should be noted that as a simple and sincere person, he gradually completes the journey of faith. In the beginning he thinks of Jesus as a "man" among others, then he considers him a "prophet," and finally his eyes are opened and he proclaims him "Lord." In opposition to the faith of the healed blind man is the hardening of the hearts of the Pharisees, who do not want to accept the miracle because they refuse to receive Jesus as the

Messiah. Instead, the crowd pauses to discuss the event and continues to be distant and indifferent. Even the blind man's parents are overcome by the fear of what others might think.

And what attitude to Jesus should we adopt? Because of Adam's sin, we too are born "blind," but in the baptismal font, we are illumined by the grace of Christ. Sin wounded humanity and destined it to the darkness of death, but the newness of life shines out in Christ, as well as the destination to which we are called. In him, reinvigorated by the Holy Spirit, we receive the strength to defeat evil and do good.

In fact, the Christian life is a continuous conformation to Christ, image of the new man, in order to reach full communion with God. The Lord Jesus is the "light of the world" (John 8:12), because in him shines "the knowledge of the glory of God" (2 Corinthians 4:6) that continues in the complex plot of the story to reveal the meaning of human existence.

In the Rite of Baptism, the presentation of the candle lit from the large paschal candle, a symbol of the risen Christ, is a sign that helps us to understand what happens in the sacrament. When our lives are enlightened by the mystery of Christ, we experience the joy of being liberated from all that threatens the full realization.

In these days that prepare us for Easter, let us rekindle within us the gift received in baptism, that flame which sometimes risks being extinguished. Let us nourish it with prayer and love for others. Let us entrust our Lenten journey to the Virgin Mary, Mother of the Church, so that all may encounter Christ, Savior of the world.

—Angelus Address, Fourth Sunday of Lent, April 3, 2011

THE MERCIFUL HEART OF THE FATHER

O n this Fourth Sunday of Lent [Cycle C], the gospel of the father and the two sons, better known as the parable of the prodigal son (Luke 15:11-32), is proclaimed. This passage of St. Luke constitutes one of the peaks of spirituality and literature of all time. Indeed, what would our culture, art, and, more generally, our civilization be without this revelation of a God the Father so full of mercy? It never fails to move us, and every time we hear or read it, it can suggest to us ever new meanings. Above all, this gospel text has the power of speaking to us of God, of enabling us to know his face, and better still, his heart.

After Jesus has told us of the merciful Father, things are no longer as they were before. We now know God; he is our Father, who out of love created us to be free and endowed us with a conscience, who suffers when we get lost and rejoices when we return. For this reason, our relationship with him is built up through events, just as it happens for every child with his parents: At first he depends on them, then he asserts his autonomy, and in the end, if he develops well, he reaches a mature relationship based on gratitude and authentic love.

In these stages we can also identify moments along man's journey in his relationship with God. There can be a phase that resembles childhood: religion prompted by need, by dependence. As man grows up and becomes emancipated, he wants to liberate himself from this submission and become free and adult—able to organize himself and make his own decisions, even thinking that he can do without God. This stage is particularly delicate and can lead to atheism, yet even this frequently conceals the need to discover God's true face. Fortunately for us, God never fails in his faithfulness. Even if we distance ourselves and get lost, he continues to follow us with his love, forgiving our errors and speaking to our conscience from within in order to call us back to him.

In this parable the sons behave in opposite ways. The younger son leaves home and sinks ever lower, whereas the elder son stays at home, but he, too, has an immature relationship with the father. In fact, when his brother comes back, the elder brother does not rejoice like the father; on the contrary, he becomes angry and refuses to enter the house. The two sons represent two immature ways of relating to God: rebellion and childish obedience. Both these forms are surmounted through the experience of mercy. Only by experiencing forgiveness, by recognizing one is loved with a freely given love—a love greater than our wretchedness but also than our own merit—do we at last enter into a truly filial and free relationship with God.

Dear friends, let us meditate on this parable. Let us compare ourselves to the two sons, and especially, let us contemplate the heart of the Father. Let us throw ourselves into his arms and be regenerated by his merciful love. May the Virgin Mary, *Mater Misericordiae,* help us to do this.

—Angelus Address, Fourth Sunday of Lent,
March 14, 2010

BE RECONCILED BY CHRIST

Dear brothers and sisters, for a fruitful celebration of Easter, the Church asks the faithful in these days to receive the Sacrament of Penance, which is like a sort of death and resurrection for each one of us. In the ancient Christian community, the bishop presided at the Rite of the Reconciliation of Penitents on Holy Thursday. Historical conditions have certainly changed, but preparing oneself for Easter with a good confession continues to be an action to make the most of. It offers us the possibility of giving our lives a fresh start and of truly having a new beginning in the joy of the Risen One and in the communion of the forgiveness that he gives us.

Aware that we are sinners but trusting in divine mercy, let us be reconciled by Christ, to enjoy more intensely the joy that he communicates with his resurrection. The forgiveness which Christ gives to us in the Sacrament of Penance is a source of interior and exterior peace; it makes us apostles of peace in a world in which divisions, suffering, and the tragedies of injustice, hatred, and violence unfortunately continue, as well as the inability to be reconciled to one another in order to start again with a sincere pardon.

However, we know that evil does not have the last word because it was the crucified and risen Christ who overcame it, and his triumph is expressed with the power of merciful love. His resurrection gives us this certainty: Despite all the darkness that exists in the world, evil does not have the last word. Sustained by this certainty, we will be able, with greater courage and enthusiasm, to commit ourselves to work for the birth of a more just world.

—General Audience, April 12, 2006

CLEANSED BY CHRIST'S LOVE

J esus purifies us through his word and his love, through the gift of himself. "You are already made clean by the word which I have spoken to you," he was to say to his disciples in the discourse on the vine (John 15:3). Over and over again, he washes us with his word.

Yes, if we accept Jesus' words in an attitude of meditation, prayer, and faith, they develop in us their purifying power. Day after day we are, as it were, covered by many forms of dirt—empty words, prejudices, reduced and altered wisdom. A multifaceted semi-falsity or falsity constantly infiltrates us deep within. All this clouds and contaminates our souls, threatening us with an incapacity for truth and the good. If we receive Jesus' words with an attentive heart, they prove to be truly cleansing—purifications of the soul, of the inner man. The gospel of the washing of the feet [John 13:1-15] invites us to this: to allow ourselves to be washed anew by this pure water; to allow ourselves to be made capable of convivial communion with God and with our brothers and sisters.

However, when Jesus was pierced by the soldier's spear, it was not only water that flowed from his side but also blood (John

19:34; cf. 1 John 5:6-8). Jesus has not only spoken; he has not left us only words. He gives us himself. He washes us with the sacred power of his blood, that is, with his gift of himself "to the end" (John 13:1), to the cross. His word is more than mere speech; it is flesh and blood "for the life of the world" (6:51). In the holy sacraments, the Lord kneels ever anew at our feet and purifies us. Let us pray to him that we may be ever more profoundly penetrated by the sacred cleansing of his love, and thereby truly purified!

—Homily, Mass of the Lord's Supper, Holy Thursday,
March 20, 2008

THE JOY OF GIVING

In inviting us to consider almsgiving with a more profound gaze that transcends the purely material dimension, Scripture teaches us that there is more joy in giving than in receiving (cf. Acts 20:35). When we do things out of love, we express the truth of our being; indeed, we have been created not for ourselves but for God and our brothers and sisters (cf. 2 Corinthians 5:15). Every time when, for love of God, we share our goods with our neighbor in need, we discover that the fullness of life comes from love, and all is returned to us as a blessing in the form of peace, inner satisfaction, and joy. Our Father in heaven rewards our almsgiving with his joy.

What is more, St. Peter includes among the spiritual fruits of almsgiving the forgiveness of sins: "Charity," he writes, "covers a multitude of sins" (1 Peter 4:8). As the Lenten liturgy frequently repeats, God offers to us sinners the possibility of being forgiven. The fact of sharing with the poor what we possess disposes us to receive such a gift. In this moment my thought turns to those who realize the weight of the evil they have committed and, precisely for this reason, feel far from God, fearful, and almost incapable of turning to him. By drawing close to others through almsgiving, we draw close to God; it can become an instrument for authentic conversion and reconciliation with him and our brothers.

—Message for Lent 2008

GIVE US A HEART OF FLESH!

B y following Jesus on the way of his passion, we not only see the passion of Jesus, but we also see all the suffering in the world, and this is the profound intention of the prayer of the Way of the Cross: to open our hearts and to help us see with our hearts.

The Fathers of the Church considered insensitivity and hardness of heart the greatest sin of the pagan world and were fond of the prophet Ezekiel's prophecy: "I will take out of your flesh the heart of stone and give you a heart of flesh" (36:26). Being converted to Christ, becoming Christian, meant receiving a heart of flesh, a heart sensitive to the passion and suffering of others.

Our God is not a remote God, intangible in his blessedness. Our God has a heart. Indeed, he has a heart of flesh; he was made flesh precisely to be able to suffer with us and to be with us in our suffering. He was made man to give us a heart of flesh and to reawaken within us love for the suffering, for the destitute.

Let us pray to the Lord at this time for all the suffering people of the world. Let us pray to the Lord that he will truly give us a heart of flesh, that he will make us messengers of his love, not only with words, but with our entire life. Amen.

—Reflection, Way of the Cross, Good Friday, April 6, 2007

GOD'S LOVE MADE VISIBLE

No one has ever seen God as he is. And yet God is not totally invisible to us; he does not remain completely inaccessible. God loved us first, says the First Letter of John (cf. 4:10), and this love of God has appeared in our midst. He has become visible in as much as he has "sent his only Son into the world, so that we might live through him" (4:9).

God has made himself visible: In Jesus we are able to see the Father (cf. John 14:9). Indeed, God is visible in a number of ways. In the love story recounted by the Bible, he comes toward us; he seeks to win our hearts, all the way to the Last Supper, to the piercing of his heart on the cross, to his appearances after the resurrection, and to the great deeds by which, through the activity of the apostles, he guided the nascent Church along its path.

Nor has the Lord been absent from subsequent Church history: He encounters us ever anew, in the men and women who reflect his presence, in his word, in the sacraments, and especially in the Eucharist. In the Church's liturgy, in her prayer, in the living community of believers, we experience the love of God; we perceive his presence, and we thus learn to recognize that presence in our daily lives. He has loved us first, and he continues to do so; we, too, then, can respond with love. God does not demand of us a feeling which we ourselves are incapable of producing. He loves us, he makes us see and experience his love; and since he has "loved us first," love can also blossom as a response within us.

—Encyclical *Deus Caritas Est*, 17

FIFTH WEEK OF LENT

*"God wants only goodness and life for us;
he provides for the health of our soul through
his ministers, delivering us from evil with
the Sacrament of Reconciliation, so that no
one may be lost."*

Fifth Sunday of Lent

JUSTICE PERSONIFIED

We have reached the Fifth Sunday of Lent, in which the liturgy this year [Cycle C] presents to us the gospel episode of Jesus who saves an adulterous woman condemned to death (John 8:1-11). While he is teaching at the Temple, the scribes and Pharisees bring to Jesus a woman caught in the act of adultery, for which Mosaic law prescribed stoning. Those men ask Jesus to judge the sinful woman in order "to test him" and impel him to take a false step. The scene is filled with drama: the life of that person, and also his own life, depend on Jesus. Indeed, the hypocritical accusers pretend to entrust the judgment to him, whereas it is actually he himself whom they wish to accuse and judge. Jesus, on the other hand, is "full of grace and truth" (John 1:14). He can read every human heart; he wants to condemn the sin but save the sinner and unmask hypocrisy.

St. John the Evangelist highlights one detail: While his accusers are insistently interrogating him, Jesus bends down and starts writing with his finger on the ground. St. Augustine notes that this gesture portrays Christ as the divine legislator: In fact, God wrote the law with his finger on tablets of stone (cf. *Commentary on John's Gospel*, 33, 5). Thus, Jesus is the Legislator, he is Justice in person. And what is his sentence? "Let him who is without sin among you be the first to throw a stone at her." These words are full of the disarming power of truth, which pulls down the wall of hypocrisy and opens consciences to a greater justice—that of love, in which consists the fulfillment of every precept (cf. Romans 13:8-10). This is the justice that also saved Saul of Tarsus, transforming him into St. Paul (cf. Philippians 3:8-14).

When his accusers "went away, one by one, beginning with the eldest," Jesus, absolving the woman of her sin, ushers her into a new life oriented to good: "Neither do I condemn you; go, and do not sin again." It is the same grace that was to make the apostle say, "One thing I do, forgetting what lies behind and straining forward to what lies ahead, I press on toward the goal for the prize of the upward call of God in Christ Jesus" (Philippians 3:13-14). God wants only goodness and life for us; he provides for the health of our soul through his ministers, delivering us from evil with the Sacrament of Reconciliation, so that no one may be lost but all may have the opportunity to convert. . . .

Dear friends, let us learn from the Lord Jesus not to judge and not to condemn our neighbor. Let us learn to be intransigent with sin (starting with our own!) and indulgent with people.

May the holy Mother of God, free from all sin, who is the mediatrix of grace for every repentant sinner, help us in this.

—Angelus Address, Fifth Sunday of Lent, March 21, 2010

RESURRECTION: THE NEW REALITY

There are only two weeks to go until Easter, and the Bible readings all speak about resurrection. It is not yet that of Jesus, which bursts in as an absolute innovation, but our own resurrection, to which we aspire and which Christ himself gave to us in rising from the dead. Indeed, death represents a wall, as it were, which prevents us from seeing beyond it. Yet our hearts reach out beyond this wall, and even though we cannot understand what it conceals, we nevertheless think about it and imagine it, expressing with symbols our desire for eternity.

The prophet Ezekiel proclaimed to the Jewish people, exiled far from the land of Israel, that God would open the graves of the dead and bring them home to rest in peace (cf. 37:12-14). This ancestral aspiration of man to be buried together with his forefathers is the longing for a "homeland," which welcomes us at the end of our earthly toil. This concept does not yet contain the idea of a personal resurrection from death, which only appears toward the end of the Old Testament and even in Jesus' time was not accepted by all Judeans. Among Christians too, faith in the resurrection and in [eternal] life is often accompanied by many doubts and much confusion because it also always concerns a reality which goes beyond the limits of our reason and requires an act of faith.

In the raising of Lazarus, we listen to the voice of faith from the lips of Martha, Lazarus' sister. Jesus says to her, "Your brother will rise again," and she replies, "I know that he will rise again in the resurrection at the last day" (John 11:23-24). But Jesus repeats: "I am the resurrection and the life; he who believes in me, though he die, yet shall he live" (11:25). This is the true newness that abounds and exceeds every border! Christ pulls down the wall of death, and in him dwells all the fullness of God, who is life—eternal life. Therefore, death did not have power over him, and the raising of Lazarus is a sign of his full dominion over physical death, which before God resembles sleep (cf. 11:11).

However, there is another death, which cost Christ the hardest struggle, even the price of the cross: It is spiritual death and sin, which threaten to ruin the existence of every human being. To overcome this death, Christ died, and his resurrection is not a return to past life but an opening to a new reality, a "new land" united at last with God's heaven. Therefore, St. Paul writes: "If the Spirit of him who raised Jesus from the dead dwells in you, he who raised Christ Jesus from the dead will give life to your mortal bodies also through his Spirit who dwells in you" (Romans 8:11).

Dear brothers and sisters, let us turn to the Virgin Mary, who previously shared in this resurrection, so that she may help us to say faithfully: "Yes, Lord; I believe that you are the Christ, the Son of God" (John 11:27), to truly discover that he is our salvation.

—Angelus Address, Fifth Sunday of Lent, April 10, 2011

The Triumph of Love

What our association with Jesus' mission consists of is explained by the Lord himself. In speaking of his forthcoming glorious death, he uses a simple and, at the same time, evocative image: "Unless a grain of wheat falls into the earth and dies, it remains alone; but if it dies, it bears much fruit" (John 12:24). He compares himself to a "grain of wheat which has split open, to bring much fruit to others," according to an effective statement of St. Athanasius. It is only through death, through the cross, that Christ bears much fruit for all the centuries. Indeed, it was not enough for the Son of God to become incarnate. To bring the divine plan of universal salvation to completion, he had to be killed and buried. Only in this way was human reality to be accepted and, through his death and resurrection, the triumph of life, the triumph of love to be made manifest: It was to be proven that love is stronger than death.

Yet the man Jesus, who was a true man with the same sentiments as ours, felt the burden of the trial and bitter sorrow at the tragic end that awaited him. Precisely because he was God-Man, he felt terror even more acutely as he faced the abyss of human sin and all that is unclean in humanity, which he had to carry with him and consume in the fire of his love. He had to carry all this with him and transform it in his love. "Now is my soul troubled," he confessed. "And what shall I say? 'Father, save me from this hour?'" (John 12:27). The temptation to ask, "Save me; do not permit the cross; give me life!" surfaces. In the distress of his invocation, we may grasp in anticipation the anguished prayer of Gethsemane when, experiencing the drama of loneliness and fear, he implored the Father to take from him the cup of the passion.

At the same time, however, his filial adherence to the divine plan does not fail, because it is precisely this that enables him to know that his hour has come, and with trust he prays, "Father, glorify your name" (John 12:28). By this he means "I accept the cross" in which the name of God is glorified—that is, the greatness of his love. Here too, Jesus anticipates the words of the Mount of Olives, the process that must be fundamentally brought about in all our prayers: to transform; to allow grace to transform our selfish will and open it to comply with the divine will.

—Homily, Fifth Sunday of Lent, March 29, 2009

LIFE IN ABUNDANCE

J esus speaks to us in the gospel, saying, "I am the resurrection and the life; he who believes in me, though he die, yet shall he live, and whoever lives and believes in me shall never die" (John 11:25).

I am the resurrection: To drink from the source of life is to enter into communion with this infinite love, which is the source of life. In encountering Christ, we enter into contact—indeed, into communion—with life itself, and we have already crossed the threshold of death, because beyond biological life we are in touch with true life.

The Church fathers have called the Eucharist a "drug of immortality." And so it is, for in the Eucharist, we come into contact—indeed, we enter into communion—with the risen Body of Christ. We enter the space of life already raised: eternal life. Let us enter into communion with this Body, which is enlivened by immortal life, and thus, from this moment and forever, we will dwell in the space of life itself.

In this way, this gospel is also a profound interpretation of what the Eucharist is, and it invites us to live truly in the Eucharist, to be able thus to be transformed into the communion of love. This is true life. In John's Gospel, the Lord says, "I came that they may have life, and have it abundantly" (10:10). Life in abundance is not as some think: to consume everything, to have all, to be able to do all that one wants. In that case we would live for inanimate things, we would live for death. Life in abundance means being in communion with true life, with infinite love. It is in this way that we truly enter into the abundance of life and also become messengers of life for others.

On their return, prisoners of war who had been in Russia for ten years or more, exposed to cold and hunger, have said: "I was able to survive because I knew I was expected. I knew that people were looking forward to my arrival, that I was necessary and awaited." This love that awaited them was the effective medicine of life against all ills. In reality, we are all awaited. The Lord waits for us; and not only does he wait for us, he is present and stretches out his hand to us.

Let us take the Lord's hand and pray to him to grant that we may truly live, live the abundance of life, and thus also be able to communicate true life to our contemporaries—life in abundance. Amen.

—Homily, Fifth Sunday of Lent, March 9, 2008

CHRIST'S EUCHARISTIC SACRIFICE

The bread I will give is my flesh, for the life of the world" (John 6:51). In these words the Lord reveals the true meaning of the gift of his life for all people. These words also reveal his deep compassion for every man and woman. The gospels frequently speak of Jesus' feelings toward others, especially the suffering and sinners (cf. Matthew 20:34; Mark 6:34; Luke 19:41). Through a profoundly human sensibility, he expresses God's saving will for all people—that they may have true life. Each celebration of the Eucharist makes sacramentally present the gift that the crucified Lord made of his life, for us and for the whole world.

In the Eucharist Jesus also makes us witnesses of God's compassion toward all our brothers and sisters. The Eucharistic mystery thus gives rise to a service of charity toward neighbor, which "consists in the very fact that, in God and with God, I love even the person whom I do not like or even know. This can only take place on the basis of an intimate encounter with God, an encounter which has become a communion of will, affecting even my feelings. Then I learn to look on this other person not simply with my eyes and my feeling, but from the perspective of Jesus Christ" (*Deus Caritas Est*, 18). In all those I meet,

I recognize brothers or sisters for whom the Lord gave his life, loving them "to the end" (John 13:1).

Our communities, when they celebrate the Eucharist, must become ever more conscious that the sacrifice of Christ is for all, and that the Eucharist thus compels all who believe in him to become "bread that is broken" for others, and to work for the building of a more just and fraternal world. Keeping in mind the multiplication of the loaves and fishes, we need to realize that Christ continues today to exhort his disciples to become personally engaged: "You yourselves, give them something to eat" (Matthew 14:16). Each of us is truly called, together with Jesus, to be bread broken for the life of the world.

—Encyclical Letter *Sacramentum Caritatis*, 88

FINDING OUR PLACE IN THE WAY OF THE CROSS

The *Via Crucis* (Way of the Cross) is neither something of the past nor of any specific point of the earth. The Lord's cross embraces the world; his *Via Crucis* crosses continents and epochs.

In the Way of the Cross, we cannot merely be spectators. We, too, are involved, so we must seek our place. Where are we?

In the Way of the Cross, it is impossible to remain neutral. Pilate, the skeptic intellectual, tried to be neutral, to remain uninvolved; but precisely in this way he took a stance against justice because of the conformism of his career. In the mirror of the cross, we have seen all the sufferings of humanity today.

In the cross of Christ, we have seen the suffering of abandoned and abused children, the threats to the family, the division of the world into the pride of the rich who do not see Lazarus at the door and the misery of the multitudes who are suffering hunger and thirst.

But we have also seen "stations" of consolation. We have seen the Mother, whose goodness stays faithful unto death and beyond death. We have seen the courageous woman [Veronica], who stood before the Lord and was not afraid to show solidarity with this Suffering One. We have seen Simon the Cyrenian, an African, who carried the cross with Jesus. Finally, we have seen, through these "stations" of consolation, that consolation, just as suffering, is never ending. . . .

So it is that we, too, are invited to find our place, to discover with these great, courageous saints the way with Jesus and for Jesus: the way of goodness and truth, the courage of love.

—Reflection, Way of the Cross, Good Friday,
April 14, 2006

CLEAN HANDS AND A PURE HEART

In [the procession of the palms], the liturgy has provided us the hymn Psalm 24. In Israel this was also a processional hymn used in the ascent to the hill of the Temple. The psalm interprets the interior ascent, of which the exterior ascent is an image, and explains to us once again what it means to ascend with Christ. "Who can ascend the mountain of the Lord?" the psalmist asks, and specifies two essential conditions. Those who ascend it and truly desire to reach the heights—to arrive at the true summit—must be people who question themselves about God. They must be people who scan their surroundings seeking God, seeking his face.

Dear young friends, how important precisely this is today: not merely to let oneself be taken here and there in life, not to be satisfied with what everyone else thinks and says and does, but to probe God and to seek God, not letting the question about God dissolve in our souls, desiring what is greater, desiring to know him—his face. . . .

The other very concrete condition for the ascent is this: He "who has clean hands and a pure heart" can stand in the holy place (Psalm 24:4). Clean hands are hands that are not used for acts of violence. They are hands that are not soiled with corruption, with bribery. A pure heart—when is the heart pure? A heart is pure when it does not pretend and is not stained with lies and hypocrisy, a heart that remains transparent like spring water because it is alien to duplicity. A heart is pure when it does not estrange itself with the drunkenness of pleasure, a heart in which love is true and is not only a momentary passion. Clean hands and a pure heart: If we walk with Jesus, we ascend and find the purification that truly brings us to that height to which man is destined—friendship with God himself.

—Homily, Palm Sunday of the Passion of Our Lord,
April 1, 2007

HOLY WEEK

*"Recognizing Jesus as King means accepting
him as the One who shows us the way, in
whom we trust and whom we follow."*

PROFESSING THE KINGSHIP OF JESUS

I n the Palm Sunday procession, we join with the crowd of disciples who in festive joy accompany the Lord during his entry into Jerusalem. Like them, we praise the Lord with a loud voice for all the miracles we have seen. Yes, we too have seen and still see today the wonders of Christ: how he brings men and women to renounce the comforts of their lives and devote themselves totally to the service of the suffering; how he gives men and women the courage to oppose violence and deceit, to make room for truth in the world; how, in secret, he persuades men and women to do good to others, to bring about reconciliation where there had been hatred and to create peace where enmity had reigned.

The procession is first and foremost a joyful witness that we bear to Jesus Christ, in whom the Face of God became visible to us, and thanks to whom the Heart of God is open to us. In Luke's Gospel the account of the beginning of the procession in the vicinity of Jerusalem is in part modeled literally on the rite of coronation with which, according to the First Book of Kings, Solomon was invested as heir to David's kingship (cf.1:33-40).

Thus, the procession of the palms is also a procession of Christ the King: We profess the kingship of Jesus Christ; we recognize Jesus as the Son of David, the true Solomon, the King of peace and justice. Recognizing him as King means accepting him as the One who shows us the way, in whom we trust and whom we follow. It means accepting his word day after day as a valid criterion for our life. It means seeing in him the authority to which we submit. We submit to him because his authority is the authority of the truth.

—Homily, Palm Sunday of the Passion of Our Lord,
April 1, 2007

THE CROSS: UNLIMITED HOPE

Many might be tempted to ask why we Christians celebrate an instrument of torture, a sign of suffering, defeat, and failure. It is true that the cross expresses all these things. And yet, because of him who was lifted up on the cross for our salvation, it also represents the definitive triumph of God's love over all the evil in the world.

There is an ancient tradition that the wood of the cross was taken from a tree planted by Adam's son, Seth, over the place where Adam was buried. On that very spot, known as Golgotha, the place of the skull, Seth planted a seed from the tree of the knowledge of good and evil, the tree in the midst of the Garden of Eden. Through God's providence, the work of the evil one would be undone by turning his own weapons against him.

Beguiled by the serpent, Adam had forsaken his filial trust in God and sinned by biting into the fruit of the one tree in the garden that was forbidden to him. In consequence of that sin, suffering and death came into the world. The tragic effects of sin, suffering, and death were all too evident in the history of Adam's descendants. . . .

The wood of the cross became the vehicle for our redemption, just as the tree from which it was fashioned had occasioned the fall of our first parents. Suffering and death, which had been a consequence of sin, were to become the very means by which sin was vanquished. The innocent Lamb was slain on the altar of the cross, and yet from the immolation of the victim, new life burst forth: The power of evil was destroyed by the power of self-sacrificing love.

The cross, then, is something far greater and more mysterious than it at first appears. It is indeed an instrument of torture, suffering, and defeat, but at the same time it expresses the complete transformation, the definitive reversal of these evils: That is what makes it the most eloquent symbol of hope that the world has ever seen. It speaks to all who suffer—the oppressed, the sick, the poor, the outcast, the victims of violence—and it offers them hope that God can transform their suffering into joy, their isolation into communion, their death into life. It offers unlimited hope to our fallen world.

—Homily at the Church of the Holy Cross,
Nicosia, Cyprus, June 5, 2010

CHRIST, VICTIM AND PRIEST

In the Eucharist Jesus anticipated his sacrifice, a non-ritual but a personal sacrifice. At the Last Supper, his actions were prompted by that "eternal Spirit" with which he was later to offer himself on the cross (cf. Hebrews 9:14). Giving thanks and blessing, Jesus transforms the bread and the wine. It is divine love that transforms them: the love with which Jesus accepts, in anticipation, to give the whole of himself for us. This love is nothing other than the Holy Spirit, the Spirit of the Father and of the Son, who consecrates the bread and the wine and changes their substance into the Body and Blood of the Lord, making present in the sacrament the same sacrifice that is fulfilled in a bloody way on the cross.

We may therefore conclude that Christ is a true and effective priest because he was filled with the power of the Holy Spirit; he was filled with the whole fullness of God's love, and precisely "in the night on which he was betrayed," precisely "in the hour . . . of darkness" (cf. Luke 22:53). It is this divine power, the same power that brought about the incarnation of the Word, that transformed the extreme violence and extreme injustice into a supreme act of love and justice. This is the work of the priesthood of Christ that the Church has inherited and extended in history, in the dual form of the common priesthood of the baptized and the ordained priesthood of ministers, in order to transform the world with God's love. Let us all, priests and faithful, nourish ourselves with the same Eucharist; let us all prostrate ourselves to adore it, because in it our Master and Lord is present, the true Body of Jesus is present in it, the Victim and the Priest, the salvation of the world. Come, let us exult with joyful songs! Come, let us adore him! Amen.

—Homily, Solemnity of Corpus Christi, June 3, 2010

THE BATTLE BETWEEN
LIGHT AND DARKNESS

In today's liturgy the Evangelist Matthew presents for our meditation the brief dialogue between Jesus and Judas that took place in the Upper Room. "Is it I, Master?" the traitor asked the divine Teacher, who had foretold, "Truly, I say to you, one of you will betray me." The Lord's answer was incisive: "You have said so" (cf. Matthew 26:14-25).

For his part, John concludes the narrative announcing Judas' betrayal with a few portentous words: "It was night" (John 13:30).

When the traitor left the Upper Room, thick darkness gathered in his heart—it was an inner night; bewilderment increased in the hearts of the other disciples—they, too, were moving toward night; while the steadily darkening twilight of abandonment and hatred hung over the Son of Man, who was preparing to consummate his sacrifice on the cross.

What we shall be commemorating in the coming days is the supreme battle between light and darkness, between life and death. We must also put ourselves in this context, aware of our own "night," of our sins and our responsibility, if we want to benefit spiritually from the paschal mystery, if we want our hearts to be enlightened through this mystery, which constitutes the central fulcrum of our faith.

—General Audience, Wednesday of Holy Week,
April 4, 2007

THE BASIN OF LOVE

Having loved his own who were in the world, he loved them to the end" (John 13:1). God loves his creature, man; he even loves him in his fall and does not leave him to himself. He loves him to the end. He is impelled with his love to the very end, to the extreme: He came down from his divine glory.

He cast aside the raiment of his divine glory and put on the garb of a slave. He came down to the extreme lowliness of our fall. He kneels before us and carries out for us the service of a slave: He washes our dirty feet so that we might be admitted to God's banquet and be made worthy to take our place at his table—something that on our own we neither could nor would ever be able to do.

God is not a remote God, too distant or too great to be bothered with our trifles. Since God is great, he can also be concerned with small things. Since he is great, the soul of man, the same man, created through eternal love, is not a small thing but great, and worthy of God's love.

God's holiness is not merely an incandescent power before which we are obliged to withdraw, terrified. It is a power of love, and therefore a purifying and healing power. God descends and becomes a slave; he washes our feet so that we may come to his table. In this, the entire mystery of Jesus Christ is expressed. In this, what redemption means becomes visible. The basin in which he washes us is his love, ready to face death. Only love has that purifying power, which washes the grime from us and elevates us to God's heights.

The basin that purifies us is God himself, who gives himself to us without reserve—to the very depths of his suffering and his death. He is ceaselessly this love that cleanses us; in the sacraments of purification—Baptism and the Sacrament of Penance—he is continually on his knees at our feet and carries out for us the service of a slave, the service of purification, making us capable of God. His love is inexhaustible; it truly goes to the very end.

—Homily, Mass of the Lord's Supper, Holy Thursday,
April 13, 2006

THE TRUTH OF GOOD FRIDAY

Let us direct our gaze today toward Christ. Let us pause to contemplate his cross. The cross is the source of immortal life, the school of justice and peace, the universal patrimony of pardon and mercy. It is permanent proof of an oblative and infinite love that brought God to become man, vulnerable like us, even to dying crucified. His nailed arms are open to each human being, and they invite us to draw near to him, certain that he accepts us and clasps us in an embrace of infinite tenderness: "I, when I am lifted up from the earth, will draw all men to myself" (John 12:32).

Through the sorrowful way of the cross, men and women of all ages, reconciled and redeemed by Christ's blood, have become friends of God, sons and daughters of the heavenly Father. "Friend" is what Jesus calls Judas, and he offers him the last and dramatic call to conversion. He calls each of us friend because he is the true friend of everyone. Unfortunately, we do not always manage to perceive the depth of this limitless love that God has for his creatures. For him there is no distinction of race or culture. Jesus Christ died to liberate the whole of humanity from ignorance of God, from the circle of hate and vengeance, from the slavery to sin. The cross makes us brothers and sisters.

Let us ask ourselves: But what have we done with this gift? What have we done with the revelation of the face of God in Christ, with the revelation of God's love that conquers hate? Many, in our age as well, do not know God and cannot find him in the crucified Christ. Many are in search of a love or a liberty that excludes God. Many believe they have no need of God. . . .

Let us allow his sacrifice on the cross to question us. Let us permit him to put our human certainties in crisis. Let us open our hearts to him. Jesus is the truth that makes us free to love. Let us not be afraid: Upon dying, the Lord saved sinners, that is, all of us. The apostle Peter wrote: Jesus "himself bore our sins in his body on the tree, that we might die to sin and live to righteousness. By his wounds you have been healed" (1 Peter 2:24). This is the truth of Good Friday: On the cross the Redeemer has restored to us the dignity that belongs to us, has made us adoptive sons and daughters of God whom he has created in his image and likeness. Let us remain, then, in adoration before the cross. O Christ, Crucified King, give us true knowledge of you, the joy for which we yearn, the love that fills our heart, thirsty for the infinite.

—Address, Way of the Cross, Good Friday,
March 21, 2008

THE SACRAMENT OF ILLUMINATION

Gregory of Tours (fourth century) recounts a practice that in some places was preserved for a long time, of lighting the new fire for the celebration of the Easter Vigil directly from the sun, using a crystal. Light and fire, so to speak, were received anew from heaven, so that all the lights and fires of the year could be kindled from them.

This is a symbol of what we are celebrating in the Easter Vigil. Through his radical love for us, in which the heart of God and the heart of man touched, Jesus Christ truly took light from heaven and brought it to the earth—the light of truth and the fire of love that transform man's being. He brought the light, and now we know who God is and what God is like. Thus, we also know what our human situation is: what we are and for what purpose we exist. When we are baptized, the fire of this light is brought down deep within ourselves. Thus, in the early Church, Baptism was also called the Sacrament of Illumination. God's light enters into us; thus, we ourselves become children of light.

We must not allow this light of truth that shows us the path to be extinguished. We must protect it from all the forces that seek to eliminate it so as to cast us back into darkness regarding God and ourselves. Darkness, at times, can seem comfortable.

I can hide and spend my life asleep. Yet we are called not to darkness but to light.

In our baptismal promises, we rekindle this light, so to speak, year by year. Yes, I believe that the world and my life are not the product of chance but of eternal Reason and eternal Love; they are created by almighty God. Yes, I believe that in Jesus Christ, in his incarnation, in his cross and resurrection, the face of God has been revealed; that in him God is present in our midst; he unites us and leads us toward our goal, toward eternal Love. Yes, I believe that the Holy Spirit gives us the word of truth and enlightens our hearts; I believe that in the communion of the Church, we all become one body with the Lord, and thus we encounter his resurrection and eternal life. The Lord has granted us the light of truth. This light is also fire, a powerful force coming from God, a force that does not destroy but seeks to transform our hearts so that we truly become men of God and so that his peace can become active in this world.

—Homily, Easter Vigil, March 22, 2008

OCTAVE OF EASTER

*"But Christ is risen, he is alive, and he walks
with us. For this reason, we sing and we walk,
faithfully carrying out our task in this world
with our gaze fixed on heaven."*

THE RADIANCE OF CHRIST'S
RESURRECTION

Easter morning brings us news that is ancient yet ever new: Christ is risen! The echo of this event, which issued forth from Jerusalem twenty centuries ago, continues to resound in the Church, deep in whose heart lives the vibrant faith of Mary, Mother of Jesus, the faith of Mary Magdalene and the other women who first discovered the empty tomb, and the faith of Peter and the other apostles.

Right down to our own time—even in these days of advanced communications technology—the faith of Christians is based on that same news, on the testimony of those sisters and brothers who saw first, the stone that had been rolled away from the empty tomb and, then, the mysterious messengers who testified that Jesus, the Crucified, was risen. And then Jesus himself, the Lord and Master, living and tangible, appeared to Mary Magdalene, to the two disciples on the road to Emmaus, and finally to all eleven, gathered in the Upper Room (cf. Mark 16:9-14).

The resurrection of Christ is not the fruit of speculation or mystical experience; it is an event that, while it surpasses history, nevertheless happens at a precise moment in history and leaves an indelible mark upon it. The light that dazzled the guards keeping watch over Jesus' tomb has traversed time and space. It is a different kind of light, a divine light that has rent asunder the darkness of death and has brought to the world the splendor of God, the splendor of Truth and Goodness.

Just as the sun's rays in springtime cause the buds on the branches of the trees to sprout and open up, so the radiance that streams forth from Christ's resurrection gives strength and meaning to every human hope, to every expectation, wish, and plan. Hence, the entire cosmos is rejoicing today, caught up in the springtime of humanity, which gives voice to creation's silent hymn of praise. The Easter Alleluia, resounding in the Church as she makes her pilgrim way through the world, expresses the silent exultation of the universe and, above all, the longing of every human soul that is sincerely open to God, giving thanks to him for his infinite goodness, beauty, and truth.

"In your resurrection, O Christ, let heaven and earth rejoice." To this summons to praise, which arises today from the heart of the Church, the "heavens" respond fully: The hosts of angels, saints, and blessed souls join with one voice in our exultant song. In heaven all is peace and gladness. But alas, it is not so on earth! Here, in this world of ours, the Easter Alleluia still contrasts with the cries and laments that arise from so many painful situations: deprivation, hunger, disease, war, violence. Yet it was for this that Christ died and rose again! He died on account of sin, including ours today; he rose for the redemption of history, including our own. So my message today is intended for everyone and, as a prophetic proclamation, it is intended especially for peoples and communities who are undergoing a time of suffering, that the risen Christ may open up for them the path of freedom, justice, and peace. . . .

May heaven and earth rejoice at the witness of those who suffer opposition and even persecution for their faith in Jesus Christ. May the proclamation of his victorious resurrection deepen their courage and trust.

Dear brothers and sisters! The risen Christ is journeying ahead of us toward the new heavens and the new earth (cf. Revelation 21:1), in which we shall all finally live as one family, as sons of the same Father. He is with us until the end of time. Let us walk behind him in this wounded world, singing "Alleluia." In our hearts there is joy and sorrow, on our faces there are smiles and tears. Such is our earthly reality. But Christ is risen, he is alive, and he walks with us. For this reason, we sing and we walk, faithfully carrying out our task in this world with our gaze fixed on heaven.

—*Urbi et Orbi* Message, Easter 2011

MY LORD AND MY GOD!

M y Lord and my God!" (John 20:28). We too renew that profession of faith of Thomas. I have chosen these words for my Easter greetings this year because humanity today expects from Christians a renewed witness to the resurrection of Christ; it needs to encounter him and to know him as true God and true man. If we can recognize in this apostle the doubts and uncertainties of so many Christians today, the fears and disappointments of many of our contemporaries, with him we can also rediscover with renewed conviction faith in Christ dead and risen for us. This faith, handed down through the centuries by the successors of the apostles, continues on because the risen Lord dies no more. He lives in the Church and guides it firmly toward the fulfillment of his eternal design of salvation.

We may all be tempted by the disbelief of Thomas. Suffering, evil, injustice, death, especially when it strikes the innocent, such as children who are victims of war and terrorism, of sickness and hunger—does not all of this put our faith to the test? Paradoxically, the disbelief of Thomas is most valuable to us in these cases because it helps to purify all false concepts of God and leads us to discover his true face: the face of a God who, in

Christ, has taken upon himself the wounds of injured humanity. Thomas has received from the Lord, and has in turn transmitted to the Church, the gift of a faith put to the test by the passion and death of Jesus and confirmed by meeting him risen. His faith was almost dead but was born again thanks to his touching the wounds of Christ, those wounds that the Risen One did not hide but showed, and continues to point out to us in the trials and sufferings of every human being.

"By his wounds you have been healed" (1 Peter 2:24). This is the message Peter addressed to the early converts. Those wounds that in the beginning were an obstacle for Thomas's faith, being a sign of Jesus' apparent failure, those same wounds have become in his encounter with the Risen One signs of a victorious love. These wounds that Christ has received for love of us help us to understand who God is and to repeat, "My Lord and my God!" Only a God who loves us to the extent of taking upon himself our wounds and our pain, especially innocent suffering, is worthy of faith.

—*Urbi et Orbi* Message, Easter 2007

ALLELUIA! REJOICE!

After the days of Lent, the singing of the "Alleluia"—a Hebrew word known across the world that means "Praise the Lord"—rings out once again. During the days of Eastertide, this invitation spreads by word of mouth, from heart to heart. It reechoes an absolutely new event: Christ's death and resurrection. The "alleluia" welled up in the hearts of Jesus' first disciples, men and women, on that Easter morning in Jerusalem. . . . It almost seems as though we hear their voices: that of Mary of Magdala, who was the first to see the risen Lord in the garden near Calvary; the voices of the women who met him as they ran, fearful but happy, to tell the disciples the news of the empty tomb; the voices of the two disciples who had set out for Emmaus with gloomy faces and returned to Jerusalem in the evening, filled with joy at having heard his words and recognizing him "in the breaking of the bread" (Luke 24:35); the voices of the eleven apostles who on that same evening saw the Lord appearing in their midst in the Upper Room, showing them the wounds of the nails and spear and saying to them, "Peace be with you" (24:36). This experience engraved the "alleluia" in the Church's heart once and for all!

From this experience too stems the *Regina Caeli*, the prayer that we recite instead of the Angelus today and every day in the Easter season. The text that replaces the Angelus in these weeks is brief and has the direct form of an announcement: It is like a new "annunciation" to Mary, this time not made by an angel but by us Christians who invite the Mother to rejoice because her Son, whom she carried in her womb, is risen as he promised. Indeed, "rejoice" was the first word that the heavenly messenger addressed to the Virgin in Nazareth. And this is what it meant: "Rejoice, Mary, because the Son of God is about to become man within you." Now, after the drama of the passion, a new invitation to rejoice rings out: "*Gaude et laetare, Virgo Maria, alleluia, quia surrexit Dominus vere, alleluia*"—"Rejoice and be glad, O Virgin Mary, alleluia. Rejoice because the Lord is truly risen, alleluia!"

Dear brothers and sisters, let us allow the paschal "alleluia" to be deeply impressed within us too, so that it is not only a word in certain external circumstances but is expressed in our own lives, the lives of people who invite everyone to praise the Lord and do so with their behavior as "risen" ones. "Pray the Lord for us," we say to Mary, that the One who restored joy to the whole world by means of his Son's resurrection may grant us to enjoy such gladness now and always, in our life and in the life without end.

—*Regina Caeli* Address, Monday in the Octave of Easter, March 24, 2008

Wednesday within the Octave of Easter

The Risen Lord Walks beside Us

Especially in this Octave of Easter, the liturgy invites us to meet the Risen One personally and to recognize his life-giving action in the events of history and in our daily lives. This Wednesday, for example, the moving episode of the two disciples of Emmaus is presented to us once again (cf. Luke 24:13-35). After Jesus' crucifixion, immersed in sadness and disappointment, they were going home dejected. On their way they discussed the events that had occurred in those days in Jerusalem; it was then that Jesus approached and began to talk to them and teach them: "O foolish men, and slow of heart to believe all that the prophets have spoken! Was it not necessary that the Christ should suffer these things and enter into his glory?" (24:25-26). Then, starting with Moses and all the prophets, he explained to them what referred to him in all the Scriptures.

Christ's teaching—the explanation of the prophecies—was like an unexpected revelation to the disciples of Emmaus, enlightening and comforting. Jesus gave them a new key for interpreting the Bible, and everything then appeared clear, oriented to that very moment. Won over by the words of the unknown wayfarer, they invited him to stop and have supper with them. And he accepted and sat down to table with them. The Evangelist Luke says, "When he was at table with them, he took the bread and blessed, and broke it, and gave it to them" (24:30). And it was at that very moment that the eyes of the two disciples were opened and they recognized him, but "he vanished out of their sight" (24:31). And full of wonder and joy, they commented, "Did not our hearts burn within us while he talked to us on the road, while he opened to us the scriptures?" (24:32).

Throughout the liturgical year, particularly in Holy Week and Easter Week, the Lord walks beside us and explains the Scriptures to us and makes us understand this mystery: Everything speaks of him. And this should also make our hearts burn within us so that our eyes, too, may be opened. The Lord is with us; he shows us the true path.

Just as the two disciples recognized Jesus in the breaking of the bread, so today, in the breaking of the bread, let us, too, recognize his presence. The disciples of Emmaus recognized him and remembered the times when Jesus had broken the bread. And this breaking of the bread reminds us of the first Eucharist celebrated in the context of the Last Supper, when Jesus broke the bread and thus anticipated his death and resurrection by giving himself to the disciples. Jesus also breaks bread with us and for us; he makes himself present with us in the Holy Eucharist; he gives us himself and opens our hearts. In the Holy Eucharist, in the encounter with his word, we too can meet and know Jesus at this twofold table of the word and of the consecrated bread and wine. Every Sunday the community thus relives the Lord's Passover and receives from the Savior his testament of love and brotherly service.

Dear brothers and sisters, may the joy of these days strengthen our faithful attachment to the crucified and risen Christ. Above all, may we let ourselves be won over by the fascination of his resurrection. May Mary help us to be messengers of the light and joy of Easter for all our brethren.

—General Audience, Wednesday in the Octave of Easter,
March 26, 2008

It's Always Easter

It is fundamental for our faith and for our Christian witness to proclaim the resurrection of Jesus of Nazareth as a real historical event, attested by many authoritative witnesses. We assert this forcefully because in our day, too, there are plenty of people who seek to deny its historicity, reducing the gospel narrative to a myth, to a "vision" of the apostles, taking up and presenting old and already worn-out theories as new and scientific.

For Jesus, of course, the resurrection was not a simple return to his former life. Should this have been the case, in fact, it would have been something of the past: Two thousand years ago someone—such as, for example, Lazarus—was raised and returned to his former life. The resurrection is placed in another dimension: It is the passage to a profoundly new dimension of life that also concerns us, that involves the entire human family, history, and the universe. This event that introduced a new dimension of life, an opening of this world of ours to eternal life, changed the lives of the eyewitnesses, as the gospel accounts and the other New Testament writings demonstrate. It is a proclamation that entire generations of men and women down the centuries have accepted with faith and to which they have borne witness, often at the price of their blood, knowing that in this very way, they were entering into this new dimension of life.

This year too, at Easter, this good news rings out unchanged and ever new in every corner of the earth: Jesus who died on the cross is risen; he lives in glory because he has defeated the power of death; he has brought the human being to a new communion of life with God and in God. This is the victory of Easter, our salvation! And therefore we can sing with St. Augustine, "Christ's resurrection is our hope!" because it introduces us into a new future. . . .

Dear brothers and sisters, let us allow ourselves to be illumined by the splendor of the risen Lord. Let us welcome him with faith and adhere generously to his gospel, as did the privileged witnesses of his resurrection, and as some years later did St. Paul, who encountered the divine Teacher in an extraordinary manner on the road to Damascus. We cannot keep for ourselves alone the proclamation of this Truth that changes the life of all. And with humble trust, let us pray: "Jesus, who in rising from the dead anticipated our resurrection, we believe in you!" I would like to end with an exclamation that Sylvan of Mount Athos used to like to repeat: "Rejoice my soul. It is always Easter, for the risen Christ is our resurrection!"

—General Audience, Wednesday in the Octave of Easter,
April 15, 2009

THE RESURRECTION:
A FUNDAMENTAL TRUTH

In the Easter season, the liturgy offers us manifold incentives to strengthen our faith in the risen Christ. . . . For example, St. Luke tells how the two disciples of Emmaus, after recognizing him "in the breaking of the bread" (24:35), returned to Jerusalem full of joy to tell the others what had happened to them.

And just as they were speaking, the Lord appeared, showing them his hands and his feet with the signs of the passion. Then, in the face of the apostles' disbelief and wonder, Jesus had them give him some broiled fish and ate it before their eyes (cf. Luke 24:35-43).

In this and in other accounts, one can discern a repeated invitation to overcome incredulity and believe in Christ's resurrection, since his disciples are called to be witnesses precisely of this extraordinary event.

The resurrection of Christ is central to Christianity. It is a fundamental truth to be reasserted vigorously in every epoch, since to deny it, as has been and continues to be attempted, or to transform it into a purely spiritual event is to thwart our very faith. St.

Paul states, "If Christ has not been raised, then our preaching is in vain and your faith is in vain" (1 Corinthians 15:14).

In the days that followed the Lord's resurrection, the apostles stayed together, comforted by Mary's presence, and after the ascension, they persevered with her in prayerful expectation of Pentecost. Our Lady was a mother and teacher to them, a role that she continues to play for Christians of all times. . . .

Let us entrust to Mary the needs of the Church and of the whole world, especially at this time, which is marked by so many shadows, . . . [and] turn to her with the prayer of the *Regina Caeli,* a prayer that enables us to taste the comforting joy of the risen Christ's presence.

—*Regina Caeli* Address, Third Sunday of Easter,
April 30, 2006

"I Am Risen and I Am with You Always"

In these days of Easter, we shall often hear Jesus' words resound: "I am risen and I am with you always." Echoing this good news, the Church proclaims exultantly: "Yes, we are certain! The Lord is truly risen, alleluia! The power and the glory are his, now and forever." The whole Church rejoices, expressing her sentiments by singing, "This is the day of our Lord Jesus Christ."

In fact, in rising from the dead, Jesus inaugurated his eternal day and has opened the door to our joy too. "I will not die," he says, "but will have everlasting life." The crucified Son of man, the stone rejected by the builders, has now become the solid foundation of the new spiritual edifice which is the Church, his mystical body. The People of God, which has Christ as its invisible head, is destined to grow in the course of the centuries until the complete fulfillment of the plan of salvation. Then the whole of humanity will be incorporated into him, and every existing reality will be penetrated with his total victory. Then, as St. Paul writes, he will be "the fullness of him who fills all in all" (Ephesians 1:23) and "God may be everything to every one" (1 Corinthians 15:28).

Thus, it is right for the Christian community to rejoice—all of us—because the resurrection of the Lord assures us that the divine plan of salvation, despite all the obscurity of history, will certainly be brought about. This is why his Passover truly is our hope. And we, risen with Christ through baptism, must now follow him faithfully in holiness of life, advancing toward the eternal Passover, sustained by the knowledge that the difficulties, struggles, and trials of human life, including death, henceforth can no longer separate us from him and his love. His resurrection has formed a bridge between the world and eternal life over which every man and every woman can cross to reach the true goal of our earthly pilgrimage.

"I am risen and I am with you always." This assurance of Jesus is realized above all in the Eucharist; it is in every Eucharistic celebration that the Church and every one of her members experience his living presence and benefit from the full richness of his love. In the Sacrament of the Eucharist, the risen Lord is present and mercifully purifies us from our sins; he nourishes us spiritually and infuses us with strength to withstand the harsh trials of life and the fight against sin and evil. He is the sturdy support in our pilgrimage toward the eternal dwelling place in heaven. May the Virgin Mary, who experienced beside her divine Son every phase of his mission on earth, help us to welcome with faith the gift of Easter and make us faithful and joyful witnesses of the risen Lord.

—*Regina Caeli* Address, Monday in the Octave of Easter, April 13, 2009

MERCY AND DIVINE GOODNESS

This Sunday concludes the Octave of Easter. It is a unique day "made by the Lord," distinguished by the outstanding event of the resurrection and the joy of the disciples at seeing Jesus. Since antiquity this Sunday has been called "*in albis*" from the Latin name, "*alba,*" which was given to the white vestments the neophytes put on for their baptism on Easter night and took off eight days later, that is, today. Venerable [now Blessed] John Paul II entitled this same Sunday "Divine Mercy Sunday" on the occasion of the canonization of Sr. Mary Faustina Kowalska on April 30, 2000.

The gospel passage from St. John (20:19-31) is full of mercy and divine goodness. It recounts that after the resurrection, Jesus visited his disciples, passing through the closed doors of the Upper Room. St. Augustine explains that "the shutting of doors presented no obstacle to the matter of that body, wherein the Godhead resided. He indeed could enter without their being opened, by whose birth the virginity of his mother remained inviolate" (*In ev. Jo.* 121, 4:CCL 36/7, 667); and St. Gregory the Great added that after his resurrection, the Redeemer appeared with a body by its nature incorruptible and tangible, but in a state of glory (cf. *Hom. in Evang. 21, 1:CCL* 141, 219). Jesus showed the signs of his passion even to the point of allowing Doubting Thomas to touch him; but how can a disciple possibly doubt? Actually, God's indulgence enables us to profit even from Thomas's disbelief, as well as from the believing disciples. Indeed, in touching the Lord's wounds, the hesitant disciple not only heals his own diffidence but also ours.

The visit of the Risen One is not limited to the space of the Upper Room but goes beyond it, to the point that all can receive the gift of peace and life with the "creative Breath." In fact, Jesus said twice to his disciples, "Peace be with you." And he added, "'As the Father has sent me, even so I send you.' Having said this he breathed on them, saying 'Receive the Holy Spirit. If you forgive the sins of any, they are forgiven; if you retain the sins of any, they are retained'" (John 20:21-22). This is the mission of the Church, eternally assisted by the Paraclete: to bear the good news, the joyful reality of God's merciful love, in order, as St. John says, "that you may believe that Jesus is the Christ, the Son of God, and that believing you may have life in his name" (20:31).

—*Regina Caeli* Address, April 11, 2010

the WORD
among us®
The *Spirit* of Catholic Living

This book was published by The Word Among Us. For thirty years, The Word Among Us has been answering the call of the Second Vatican Council to help Catholic laypeople encounter Christ in the Scriptures—a call reiterated by Pope Benedict XVI and a Synod of Bishops.

The name of our company comes from the prologue to the Gospel of John and reflects the vision and purpose of all of our publications: to be an instrument of the Spirit, whose desire is to manifest Jesus' presence in and to the children of God. In this way we hope to contribute to the Church's ongoing mission of proclaiming the gospel to the world and growing ever more deeply in our love for the Lord.

Our monthly devotional magazine, *The Word Among Us*, features meditations on the daily and Sunday Mass readings, and currently reaches more than one million Catholics in North America each year and another 500,000 Catholics in 100 countries. Our press division has published nearly 200 books and Bible studies over the past 12 years.

To learn more about who we are and what we publish, log on to our Web site at **www.wau.org**. There you will find a variety of Catholic resources that will help you grow in your faith.

Embrace His Word, Listen to God . . .